I0455969

2020 Vision

An Independent Strategy to Dismantle Corruption and Polarization in America

Kurt Jordan

Advanced Reading Copy
Copyright 2017

Table of Contents

Author's Perspective

I share this with you only because one's experience shapes their views and feel I should be transparent should you care. I was born in 1960 in Redondo Beach, CA, the youngest of four. My father is a mountain of a man, a child of the Depression who can still tell you how much the family earned as migrating day laborers in the 30's for a flat of berries. He tells stories of eating what they could find, including frogs and beans. At one time, the family lived in a tent. At 13, he waved goodbye to his father for the last time when his dad took an oil drilling job in the Philippines. It was Friday, June 13, 1941, and little did he realize that his father was headed into the teeth of a Japanese Juggernaut. He lost his father after 42 months as a POW of the Japanese in the Philippines. Thereafter, dad was the man of the house raised mainly by women.

My American-born mother did not speak English until she was eight from a Mexican family. When the family moved to Los Angeles from El Paso, her father insisted they abandon Spanish so as blue-eyed Hispanics; they could blend in better in a discriminatory environment. Her father was a social alcoholic, and while not physical, played a lot of emotional head games with the family, especially with the women.

My parents met on a blind date and fell in love. Dad was called to Korea where he saw a good bit of action as a combat infantryman. My mother wrote letters every day and dad wrote when he could. All those letters are in a box at my parent's home. My father was a foreman at the Chevron oil refinery and my mother was a clerk at the local water utility. We lived four blocks from the Pacific Ocean at a time when blue-collared families could afford to do so and life was too good to be true. They attended every piano recital and every little league game. No one has ever heard them raise their voices to one another, EVER! They worked hard, were honest, helped others, always paid their way, and their promise was as good as gold.

I attended Catholic school for 12 years at great sacrifice to my parents. I honored them with a GPA of 2.7 and had absolutely no other ambition than a good beach volleyball game and a hot date. Life in Redondo Beach in the 70's had a plethora of distractions and I took advantage of each and every one of them. I enrolled in a junior college and dropped out so that I would not flunk out and dad put me to work in the oil refinery. It was a very tough environment and workers were more than willing to "meet you at the gate" to kick your ass for the slightest provocation. Scared to death, reflecting on a bleak future, I re-enrolled and was a straight-A student earning acceptance into UC Berkeley as genetics major, later changing to an economics major.

Upon graduation, I interviewed wearing a brown polyester pin-striped suit, yellow cowboy boots, and enough cologne to choke a skunk. I remembered looking in the mirror just before my interview thinking, "Yep, looks sharp. Ready to go." The only call back I received was from the GE audit department who wanted to get a good laugh from their friends back at the office before they dismissed me. I ultimately accepted a math teaching position at my old Catholic high school. I put everything I had into teaching and tried to make a difference especially with lost kids like myself who needed a little push in the right direction.

I was accepted to graduate business school at Berkeley, and after graduating, was miraculously hired by Solomon Brothers, the biggest, baddest Wall Street firm at the time. I became the derivatives specialist in Atlanta and reported to the Liar's Poker team described by Michael Lewis, who was my counterpart in London. When the equity market blew up in 1987, most of my training class, including me, was let go.

I started a derivatives business at a regional bank in Atlanta that saw two mergers motivated by enriching the "boy's club" at the top and not by economics. After four years, I signed on with Lehman Brothers for another eight years and saw more of what corporate culture was all about as a Senior Vice President. After riding through some serious market dislocations during the Russian ruble crisis and a handful of morally challenging predicaments, it was clear that I no longer belonged. I rode out another four years at a boutique bond shop until I finally died the bond salesman's death, no longer having the drive to do what it takes to milk the golden cow. I had amassed a good amount of money riding the stock market up, only to get clobbered with the wave of accounting fraud and the crazy tech bubble that destroyed my portfolio in 2001.

In 2004, I was lost. I had no the energy to fight it out as a bond salesman but could not see myself in a political and bureaucratic corporate cubical being a good soldier in the "sit down, shut up, and agree with the boss" culture. I had two young kids in private school and had only enough savings to last me about 2 years with my white collared bills.

Several years ago, my wife and I had this idea for a new business and, in 2004; we started Mosquito Curtains Inc. over the garage on a shoestring with one sewing machine and a roll of fabric. It was quite a transition and the hours were absolutely insane at 90 hour weeks for the first two years, sweating as to whether or not I could build an internet business around a home improvement product. Here is an anecdote. The rolls were 12ft long and weighed 150 lbs., too big to take up the stairs. Imagine getting this roll up through a second story window at 11pm on a Sunday night working until blood dripped from your eyeballs and then heading for bed where you knew you would be up all night worrying about the future of your family. That gives you a pretty typical picture of life as an entrepreneur. That was 13 years ago and now we have a solid little business with 20 employees and growing like a weed.

Over those past 13 years, I had a lot of time to think as we would talk while cutting curtains late into the night. My world was turned upside down and I had more life experience than I really wanted, but along my journey I linked those many experiences together to try to make sense of the mysteries of American life. In fact, for the longest time, the working title of this book was "Thoughts at the Cutting Machine." We talked religion, politics, corporate America. We debated social issues, class division and even the mysteries of how men and women think differently.

During the birth of our nation the framers debated how we should be governed. Thomas Jefferson argued for a true democracy while Alexander Hamilton argued that the ordinary man was incapable of making lofty decisions that should be left to the educated aristocratic elite. Jefferson responded by saying that even the loftiest of decisions could be made by an ordinary farmer if the issues were explained in terms he could understand. Ideas should stand on their own merit and not on the credentials of the communicator. I am an ordinary man who has paid attention…and I have a lot to say.

I. Synopsis

Let me start by saying that I can't stand American Politics. You... can't stand American politics. What I hate even worse is bitching about American politics. It only riles the emotions and after a short time, I can't stand to even listen to myself. Unless someone wants to talk about feasible solutions, I kindly opt out of such discussions. I am an independent with no real home. The problem with being an independent is that there is no independent agenda. Independents are merely "not" aligned with either party's ideology, but have no cohesive direction of their own. Independents are an aimless herd of wild horses, ready to run free, but where?

The book is organized into four parts. First, we examine the nature of corruption, its characteristics, and how it has evolved within a group dynamic. Here, we establish premises for later arguments. Second, if we are to change, we need to first de-corrupt the rule makers and examine the inherent friction to change. Third, we use a Sun Tzu approach to strategy, tactics and timing to create that change. Lastly, we examine some social issues that would change absent corruption. After all, if there is no prize at the end that improves lives, why go through the trouble?

I am as ordinary a person as you would ever meet. I am not a pundit, or an academic, nor do I have an ounce of political experience or ambition. I am simply a small business owner, husband, son and father who likes to solve problems. I have a quirky way of looking at the world and make unconventional connections through my own life experiences. And before I waste another minute of your time, let's get right to the point.

For the purposes of this book, I broadly define corruption as the advancement of one's agenda by unfairly forcing a disadvantage to another by lying, cheating, stealing, fraud, coercion, or use of force.

Corruption is an athlete running a foot race who elbows his opponent so that he can win. Corruption is a welfare recipient who uses the money to take a cruise or a CEO who manipulates an obscene compensation package outside the free market. Corruption is a lobbyist who buys insensible legislation, a thief, or a rapist who ruins another's emotional life for a moment of power and gratification. Corruption lies, cheats, steals and enslaves others. In many cases, not only is corruption legal, it has been institutionalized. Drift into utopian dreamland for a moment and just imagine what our world would be like without corruption of any sort and, Wow!

Liberals and Conservatives banter stale mantras that are so old, we recite them from rote memory, no longer challenging the veracity of those mantras. We overcomplicate our arguments and dismiss opposing views as uninformed, emotional or stupid. There just might be a silver bullet that we can rally around to end senseless polarization. We only need to cooperate rationally around a simple principle that it is not okay to steal, cheat, or use power to advance ourselves at the expense of others.

When people hear the word "corruption crusader", they think conspiracy theorists who believe in a boogeyman machine that is the puppeteer of our global society. Not so! Corruption, as we define it, is as old as the hills and a natural tendency of every living animal, namely to get what we want with the least amount of effort. But while corruption may benefit those adept at using it, **corruption shrinks the pie we all eat from so that a few may wrangle a fatter unearned slice**. We as human beings have the intellect to rise above ourselves and to see ourselves as part of a larger group and to direct our behavior beyond what our natural tendencies tell us to do.

If you examine every social, economic and world issue we face today against the yardstick of corruption, the problem is crystal clear. The remedies may seem plainly obvious, but they are not. **The challenge is to reduce corruption while preserving as much individual liberty as possible and that is very difficult.** Freedom to self-determine is the same freedom that empowers corruption and separation is a very fine line.

Unfortunately, we have come to expect corruption in both politics and society. We are indignant when corrupt tactics are used against us, yet seem to have amnesia when corrupt tactics support our cause. We rationalize that we must balance corrupt forces with more justifiable corruption. Instead of attacking corruption as a disease, we manage the symptoms. Instead of a surgical strike, we carpet-bomb with broad remedies. For example, when we feel that wealth is being obtained unfairly, we attack all wealth instead of sharpshooting corruption-generated wealth.

Corruption can be considered the root of all evil in the world and manifests itself in both obvious and less obvious ways. Without corruption holding us back, we can explore possibilities of a better world. America, as great as she is, certainly is not immune from corruption and, in many cases, has managed to legalize it. Of course, **current beneficiaries of corruption do not want the rules to change**. The beneficiaries are powerful and have lulled us into complacency by dividing into a polarized battle between binary ideologies, discouraging real change in a fog of war. They will present a formidable obstacle to all attempts at changing the rules. Politics is the proverbial *head of the snake* and, despite 240 years of institutionalized corruption, can be influenced by a surprisingly small number of determined individuals with just enough critical mass to make it happen, especially if they can control the political center of gravity. Unless an Independent Movement takes a "head shot" at the political machine where rules are made, fighting for change on any particular issue is what my father would say, "Peeing up a rope." It will require a group effort with a clever strategy, persistence, and time.

The key to a good solution will be a solid universally accepted agenda consistent with our fundamental nature as human beings and our culture as Americans. For example, we know that free markets work, we know that Americans love the liberty to choose, and that we believe in self-determination with rewarded accomplishment. We are a country of both religious and secular influences and even our basic concept of right and wrong will vary widely. Self-reflection into our nature will certainly form the bedrock of a clear concise agenda; and, I will try to unite the religious and secular on common ground for a common cause.

The strategy is one that Sun Tzu would appreciate, as much is taken from his ancient handbook, *The Art of War* written 500 B.C.

Political corruption is a manifestation of a group dynamic and is a group entity in and of itself with a belief system, a set of values and even a personality. Corruption has a will to survive. If we recognize its nature, perhaps it can be dismantled. It is important to keep our eye on the ball and to not confuse the enemy. In fact, those we intuitively think are enemies may actually be allies.

I sincerely believe that many politicians would like to de-corrupt America as much as anyone; they just need a road map to do so and the right motivation. Change is always unsettling and crusaders are seldom rewarded for their efforts. The conflict of interest to a politician is obvious. After all, **who could ever expect someone holding a seat to want to change the rules of a system that gave them that seat?** There are viable strategies for removing obstacles by finding clever ways to remove resistance to change. For example, we might enact forward dated laws making the personal ramifications of change irrelevant to a sitting politician. This is not the most courageous way to do politics, but it has worked in the past and it pays to be pragmatic.

Many have tried to create an independent party as an alternative to a two-party system and all have failed to produce meaningful results. I do believe there is a viable way to create a middle voice with an Independent Movement that is quite influential *without being seduced into thinking that a bona fide independent party should necessarily be the goal.* A de facto independent movement may have far more power than an actual party if it can align its interest enough to attract influence.

Corruption is as old as man himself and is certainly nothing new. In fact, there have been considerable improvements throughout history. Imagine ancient Rome or the age of the British Empire…even things done fifty years ago would never stand today. However, this is an opportunity to make a giant leap in social evolution and set a new course by chipping away at it. The more corruption we can kill, the easier it is to kill more. The prize is that many of our social and financial issues evaporate as corruption is lessened from our lives. We are smart enough and the ample empirical evidence is clear enough that we can dramatically improve the quality of life on our planet. When we are uncertain, we can create experiments to test small, apply what is successful, and learn from failure. Special interest is an agenda that impedes our ability to move forward.

We do not have to make a change at all and can continue complaining in *quiet desperation* around the water cooler, but that is what sheep do and squarely dishonors the sacrifice other patriots have made before us. I hope you will agree that we all have a little fight in us if it is a good fight with clear feasible goals. We have a fiduciary responsibility to improve America.

This discussion is about solutions and not about complaints. **It is not about right or wrong, rather; it is about what we want and how to get it.** First, we map out premises we might agree upon. We look inward as to who we are and who we want to be. If solutions are consistent with our nature, they are more likely to work. We can search the past to look for supporting evidence as to probable outcomes of strategic possibilities. If there are obstacles to a beneficial behavior change, we examine how to overcome those obstacles and then implement a plan with the highest probability of a successful outcome.

The goal is to remove corruption from politics or at least severely curtail it. Once corruption is removed from the rule makers, the next step will to attack corruption within our American society. **It is not about taking sides on one issue or another; it is about removing corruption from influencing rational decisions.**

The time is ripe for a move in the right direction. Technology has made information readily available and communication moves at lightning speed.

Because of the internet, a ground swell has already developed. Anti-corruption groups are popping up all the time and 42% of Americans are proudly declaring themselves as Independents, or more accurately, as unaligned with either Democrats of Republicans.

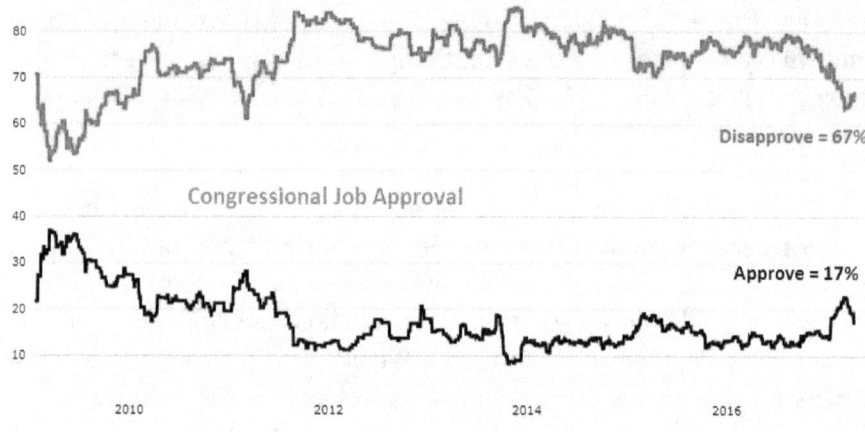

During the 2016 election, the public seemed to crave the non-establishment politicians like Bernie Sanders, Donald Trump and Ted Cruz. The public just wants change but does not quite know which direction to go. We as citizens know there is a problem but we just can't seem to put our finger on it. For that reason, have no solution agenda. **An independent movement needs to be led squarely from the middle** and cannot be led from either the far right (Ted Cruz) or the far left (Bernie Sanders) who, while campaigning for anticorruption, muddy the waters with other pet agenda items. What Conservative wants a corruption crusader with an underlying Liberal agenda and vice versa? Of course, Donald Trump has proven that the voters are so frustrated that they are willing to take a big gamble. Trump is a charismatic personality and strikes the right chord with those looking for something different, but is he the right kind of different? Many suspect that candidates will fight corruption only when it is an obstacle to their personal agendas, but embrace it when it is to their advantage. To really fight corruption, we need laser focus to make the fight a single-issue goal. First things, first, and the other issues will work out on their own when we retrieve our ability to make rational decisions in the absence of corruption.

Something is a brewing out there. The only missing ingredient is an agenda and strategies to begin making it happen by the year 2020.

II. The Fundamental Premise of Our Nature

A. What is Fair and Unfair?

As previously defined, corruption is the advancement of one's agenda by unfairly imposing a disadvantage to another such as lying, cheating, stealing, bribing, coercion or use of force. This begs the question, "What is fair?"

Secular views assume that should we all accept a God, He does not seem to get actively involved in our day to day lives to referee fair and unfair. I will grant that some may hold the view that God will referee right and wrong in the hereafter, but for whatever reason, He seems to let things play out on their own in the here and now. From a practical viewpoint, fair is what we collectively decide fair to be. We can decide the rules for wrestling are Olympic rules, WWF rules, or even gladiatorial rules depending upon what suits us. The harsh reality is that the powerful set the rules despite our efforts to feel morally elevated above the Darwinistic amorality of life.

Once upon a time, when we lived in caves, there lived a specimen of a man named Gyork who was bigger, stronger, and faster than any of the other cave dwellers. When Gyork wanted another man's woman, he clubbed him over the head and dragged her away to Gyork's harem of snatched women. A dispossessed man might feel he had been wronged but, in the end, it did not matter. Gyork still had his woman.

One night as the dispossessed bachelors sat around the fire, they began complaining about Gyork and how unhappy they were that their Neander-babes were snatched away while massaging their bruised noggins. Some had tried to retrieve their women, but were unsuccessful since Gyork had the instincts of a cat. They called upon the sun god whom Gyork seemed to respect but it did no good. Some even tried to reason with Gyork, but Gyork felt that as the biggest, strongest and fastest, it was his right to have any woman he wanted and went so far as to explain to them that the sun god said as much to him in a dream.

One of the cave dwellers got a bright idea. "If we band together, we

*are stronger than Gyork and can whoop his ass and get our women back."
And, so they did while banishing Gyork forever. Another cave dweller
recognized the implications that if it happened once it could happen again
and it was messy business having to defend your woman at all hours of the
day. So, they made a rule. No clubbing a man for his woman. They made
a sign and posted it on the cave, agreeing to collectively enforce the new
rule. They formed a social contract and gave up their collective right to
steal another man's woman for a greater good that seemed to benefit the
group as a whole. There was no discussion of morality over the issue.
They wanted the behavior to stop and it did, plain and simple.*

Fair is not about right or wrong. Fair is what we decide it to be!
We can argue all day long that Hitler was a bad man and that he is burning
in hell, but between 1932 and 1945, he was lord god of Germany. When
he wanted people dead, they were killed. All the complaining and morality
speeches in the world would not have changed that terrible fact. It was
only when enough of us banded together to defeat his power to make the
rules that those rules changed in Germany.

We are free to choose any set of rules we like. We can burn witches at
the stake or play Robin Hood and rob the rich on behalf of the poor. Right
and wrong on earth is determined by us, so we had better take the matter
seriously and decide what sort of world we want to live in. I happen to
think corruption is counterproductive and forces some to work harder for
the benefit of cheaters and thieves. I believe corruption prevents us from
making rational decisions as a nation and the world would be a safer
happier place without it. I do not like the idea of being robbed, cheated,
intimidated or physically attacked. I want this behavior to stop. I see no
point belaboring an argument around some absolute morality that is above
us all. There is absolutely nothing I can do to defeat corruption, alone. I
must build a consensus, form a social contract, agree on a rule, abide by it,
and enforce it with the power of a group. As Sun Tzu has explained, a
small army can defeat a much larger army with a clever strategy.

A subtle but important point of the social contract amongst the cave
dwellers was that some individual liberty was lost, namely the freedom to
steal another man's woman. At first glance this may seem trivial. After
all, why should we object to a behavior that should not be acceptable in the

first place? This is where we need to shed our pre-conceived notions – a challenge I will make throughout this book. To improve security, the cave dwellers had to yield some liberty. We must turn the knobs to create the right balance.

Change needs to be based upon principle and not on personal interest. Principle is defendable while personal interest depends upon perspective. Exceptions can and are rationalized by all of us more often than we think. Stealing cave women made perfect sense to Gyork so we can't always depend upon others to agree. Are you prepared to give up a particular interest that might apply to you? You might if the "package" is in your interest. But to "cherry pick" interest over principle is a recipe for immediate failure. The urge to cherry pick is very powerful. We have adopted ideologies that are difficult to let go. *We have been seduced with our own permission and it is worth restating that the rules are OUR choosing.*

Rules are tricky business, particularly when it applies to law. What if a cave dweller was actually a good guy stealing a woman away to protect her from an abusive spouse? Now we add conditions. If the law were irrevocable, the cave dwellers would have a dilemma.

Take free speech for example. The first amendment enables citizens to burn the American flag or the Bible. This has been the basis for Klan rallies and other unsavory acts. One problem is that free speech enables pay-to-play politics whereby lobbyists of the powerful effectively make the rules we all must abide. By accepting the right to free speech, we must accept that others will have that same right. The Supreme Court has ruled that Super PACs and other special interest are a protected right of free speech as written. As ruled in the case against *Citizens United*, paid influence of a Super PAC is perfectly legal and defended by the Constitution.

The Constitution is a brilliant document, even though the founding fathers compromised heavily to write it. Even they considered the Constitution to be an imperfect document. Yet despite its imperfection, it seems to have weathered time as its primary principles have made us what we are today. The beauty of the Constitution is that it was made not as a static document for all time but as a living breathing document that included provisions for change so it could adapt to unforeseen situations. This feature makes the constitution even more brilliant but, we have been afraid to exercise our right to amend it.

We treat the Constitution as a static document such that amending it is tantamount to sacrilegiously re-writing the Holy Bible. It has been amended seemingly only in the most extreme circumstances like abolishing slavery or giving women the right to vote. I would bet that should the founding fathers be alive today, they would have re-written it long ago by adapting to an ever-changing world. Jefferson advocated that the Constitution be revisited every 19 years by each new generation lest succeeding generations be unduly bound by the decisions of previous generations. I sincerely believe the founding fathers would have done more than we have to improve it. After all, how could someone from the 18th century ever have anticipated technological advancements like mass media, automatic weapons or the internet? It is our most precious document and should be the foundation of law; however, we have been glacially slow to allow it to adapt as it was intended to adapt. Often, those that use the Constitution to support their agenda encourage us to see it as a static document. But since the rules of society are dictated by the powerful and we all have the means to form our own collective armies of influence for a given cause, everything is on the table for negotiation.

B.   Political World Views

Imagine you are a marriage counselor. You first spend an hour with each spouse individually. They are both likeable people with a set of values that seem to have a consistent logic to them, but when it is time for both to be in session together, all hell breaks loose. They enter the room and sit as far away from each other on the couch as humanly possible. After listening to the two bicker back and forth for an hour, your takeaway is that while they are both good people with the best intentions, there is a subtext cartoon bubble over their heads that says the exact same thing, "If she or he just saw the world the way I do, we would not be sitting here." What seemed to be two perfectly rational adults now reveal significant inconsistencies in their expectations.

She says, "I love that he's a good provider, but he's too single-minded and always seems distracted when he comes home late and we never go out any more. I just do not feel cared for." He says, "She's a great mom and homemaker, but why is she up my tail feathers whenever I leave a dirty dish. I just do not feel appreciated after a hard day's work." If have ever read John Gray's *Men are From Mars, Women are From Venus*, you will get that men and women are simply wired differently. Being a good provider requires a certain singlemindedness, and unless you are superman, at the end of a hard day you are often spent and emotionally unavailable. Being a good homemaker also requires super powers and the last thing you need is for the kids, you are teaching to clean up after themselves, to see their father, the only adult interaction you will have that day, break all the rules and go off to bed alone.   Both have critical roles in the family unit, but unless they can recognize each other's view point, you will find more discord than cooperation.

What is exceptionally fortunate in our democracy is that we have both liberal and conservative viewpoints, just as a family benefits from opposing viewpoints. It is fortunate BECAUSE their values are prioritized differently that those differences create both balance and conflict. Too much of one and not enough of the other is not healthy for a family or a nation. Conflict simply paralyzes any progress. We all want to feel safe, see our children prosper, worry less, and scratch out a little happiness for ourselves. We just understand those ideals very differently.

Fundamental Liberal and Conservative Values

Conservatives have an emphasis on laws, institutions, customs and religion Conservatives recognize that democracy is a huge achievement and that maintaining the social order requires imposing constraints on people. Conservatives like what is familiar to them and resist the uncertainty of too much change too quickly. Conservatives value patriotism, stoicism, security, self-reliance, order, rewarded accomplishment, immediate effects, and moral purity. From his book, *Moral Politics*, George Lakoff states that in political discussions, conservatives will use words such as:

character, virtue, discipline, tough it out, get tough, tough love, strong, self-reliance, individual responsibility, backbone, standards, authority, heritage, competition, earn, hard work, enterprise, property rights, reward, freedom, intrusion, interference, meddling, punishment, human nature, traditional, common sense, dependency, self-indulgent, elite, quotas, breakdown, corrupt, decay, rot, degenerate, deviant, lifestyle.

Liberal values, on the other hand, emphasize values that ensure that the rights of weaker members of society are respected; limiting harmful environmental effects, and fostering innovation. Liberals are more comfortable with the unfamiliar and are comfortable with change. Liberals emphasize fairness, equality, social justice, long term benefits, the environment, and protecting the vulnerable. They will use words such as:

social forces, social responsibility, free expression, human rights, equal rights, concern, care, help, health, safety, nutrition, basic human dignity, oppression, diversity, deprivation, alienation, big corporations, corporate welfare, ecology, ecosystem, biodiversity, pollution, and so on.

All are worthy values and are shared values to some extent but are emphasized differently. Our values make us feel safer and make us believe we will all have a better chance to be happy. They form the foundation of how the two groups view the role of government. Liberals and Conservatives differ on how they prioritize these values and what those values mean.

For example, everyone wants to feel safe. Conservatives feel safer with a strong military; they feel safer if they own a gun so that they can be responsible for their own protection. They feel safe when there is order, distinction and predictability from the rule of law. Liberals on the other hand feel safer when the motivators of crime are removed rather than self-defense with a gun. They are more inclined to rely on diplomacy over military strength. They feel safer when we all see ourselves as a big cooperative team.

We cannot dismiss opposing points of view as uninformed, unimportant, stupid, evil or subversive and expect a positive result. If these values are real to the other party, they are real enough to be taken seriously and should be addressed. If in your heart, you believe life begins at conception and that abortion is murder, you would be expected to defend the pro-life movement. If you honestly believe that life begins sometime later and that an unwanted pregnancy is emotionally and physically harmful to a mother, you would be expected to support pro-choice. Invalidation of opposing values means you have either run out of good arguments or that you were magically ordained with a monopoly on all that is true and decided it was time to pull moral rank.

Each side understandably will build their consensus and one side will win in the courts and the fight for share of mind will go on. In the meantime, one would hope that there is a mutually shared goal worth cooperating on, namely, to reduce the number of unwanted pregnancies in a rational way.

It might be hard for a liberal to hear that we are teaching abstinence to kids, but it will be equally difficult for a conservative hear that we are making condoms available to those same kids. Do we want fewer abortions or not? Do we want fewer women to be put in that position or not? If this idea bristles your feathers, ask yourself why?

We live in a nation where half are conservative and half are liberal. Not everyone is going to think like we do, so we had better get used to it. It is in the interest of liberals and conservatives to listen to each other to advance our respective agendas. Divorce is not an option since we all play in the same sandbox. We can either respect our differences and find common ground to move forward, or we can bicker like a bad marriage and go nowhere. If we simply try to jam our views down the throats of the opposition or stonewall, you can expect them to do the same. It is where we are today. **We are polarized and progress is paralyzed.**

Political Values

Political Values are presumably derived by Fundamental Values and for the most part they are. It is where we stand on political issues consistent with our highest value priorities. Sometimes, once we link a political value to a fundamental value, we know longer question the political value. For example, take the issue of Obama Care. Liberals have decided they love it and Conservatives have decided they hate it. Some no longer question why, they just do. Liberals value that the vulnerable will have reasonable access to health care. Conservatives may balk that it violates a higher value of self-reliance. Why should one person be forced to pay for another person's misfortune with their earned money? The two parties become polarized when they find inconsistencies in values. Gee Mr. Righty Right, didn't they teach you compassion in Bible class? Why yes, Mr. Lefty Left, they also taught me, thou shalt not steal, what is fair about me paying for a subsidy? And now the battle of ideology is on to the point where both feel the other is a hypocrite and stop listening.

If Liberals and Conservatives want to find common ground, they need to first understand the fundamental values from the opposition's point of view and address them in the same terms. Explaining to a conservative that people are dangerous when they feel disenfranchised and disposable might trigger the safety, order, and religious values. Explaining to liberals that wealth redistribution through some form of subsidy is dangerous to the long-term welfare of our economic ecosystem, might trigger long-term benefit and environmental values.

Political Ideology

Fundamental values probably have some origin in our neuroanatomy in that conservatives and liberals are wired differently. We all more-or-less share most fundamental values, but we prioritize them very differently and then form political values as to what role government should play to intercede, if at all. Then, we have decided on a position and no longer re-examine whether our position is the best possible solution to get us what we want. We slip into political ideology as a given that needs to be defended with all means possible and attack opposition values. More accurately, if the opposition does not prioritize values the way I do, they must not believe in the value at all. *Republicans do not want black babies to have milk for lunch while Democrats want to destroy the wholesomeness of America with another Gay Pride parade.* The good news is that Independents have questioned their loyalties. That is not to say that they do not have their own personal ideologies, they are just not aligned enough to drink the Kool-aide because they have broken away, in part, from more established polar ideologies.

This sort of polarization of political ideologies forms the seeds of corruption. We feel so rooted in our value system that we find ways to justify cheating for the sake of what we believe to be higher moral values. We need to stop, turn around, and self-examine. Both Conservatives and Liberals have terrific ideas that at some level make sense to everyone. It is our blind defense of preconceived ideologies that paralyze us into squabbles that get us nowhere.

Compromise is not in the lexicon of staunch ideologues. One cannot pontificate over ideology and then compromise without being viewed as compromising core values. Ideologues "box themselves" into all or nothing positions that contribute to polarization. Consider the very conservative Freedom Caucus. Even if they did have a better mouse trap, they cannot wag the dog from such an extreme viewpoint. Unfortunately, these voters are voting for obstructionist politicians who are simply marginalized without enough critical mass to get anything done.

Creating a Corruption Value

Quite simply, we need to elevate the value of dismantling corruption with universal values that appeal to everyone. This should be an easy task as it is so consistent with both conservative and liberal values. After all, everyone hates cheaters, liars, bullies, and thieves. The task must be described in terms of security, order, patriotism and self determination to conservatives, then to liberals in terms of equalizing, fair, innovative, socially conscious, and beneficial to the broad environment. Most important, such an effort must be led from the middle where compromise occurs between honest brokers.

It is all in how the anti-corruption value is communicated. Corruption is about power, and power is often justified to defend political views especially when we cannot seem to convince others outright. The bickering of spouses is an ugly sight when one cannot win without the other losing. The child who steps forward with wonder in her eyes to remind them that there is an affected ecosystem can often sober the belligerents.

C.   The Nature of Groups

Groups are interesting creatures that have personalities and identities of their own, with a set of values, goals and behavior that sometimes differ from those of its individual constituents. Take for example mob violence. Individuals collect together and a new personality is formed in ways that would not occur individually. Groups are entities in and of themselves with a Darwinist will to survive. Groups thrive when they grow in number and influence and are rewarded with survival through perpetuation of the group species. Groups become a footnote in history when they do not. For groups to grow, they need new members and generally money. Lots of people and lots of money equal power. Groups can form larger groups in alliances and can fight other groups by competing for new members or attacking and degrading other groups.

The main motivators for joining a group are the benefits to being inside the group or penalties for being outside the group. In Iraq during the reign of Saddam Hussein, walking talking and acting like a Baathist (Saddam ideologue), gave one privilege. If you were not, it was impossible to hold any position of importance. As a Baathist, the individual might act in ways they may not have otherwise. The negative motivator was fear of suspicion, possibly death, while privileged opportunity was the reward.

What we will do as a group can sometimes be frightening or at the very least compromise our integrity if we are not paying attention. Belonging is a strong human drive and sometimes we are willing to compromise our beliefs and behavior for the status, utility, or comradery we might cherish within a group. We might even overlook important flaws within a group for the sake of membership and the identity perks we might enjoy. Being a conservative in the Hollywood film community or a liberal in a small lily-white town in Alabama would be hard. With time, our environment will shape our views. Spend a year in the West Bank and you might come away with a different viewpoint of the Israeli-Palestinian conflict than a year spent in Tel Aviv. If you do not think you are susceptible to the influence within a group, you are kidding yourself. We all love to think we are above it all, but over time it is very difficult not to identify with those in your immediate environment to some degree.

We can control the environment we put ourselves. We can also periodically reassess who and what we are outside the groups to which we belong. Often, we isolate ourselves in groups and lose our objectivity, a quality endorsed by group entities. We tend to seek out groups that share our common interest and listen to the news we want to hear. For example, is it a surprise that Conservatives watch Fox News and Liberals watch NBC? Do you believe these media stations discourage the group think they perpetuate? What we often forget is that many of the personalities in the media are entertainers and NOT objective journalists.

Alliances we form within groups can be motivated purely by interest and not necessarily by ideology. I suspect that there are many times Republicans would love to distance themselves from the hard right as Democrats would love to distance themselves from the hard left. These are marriages of convenience based purely on utility. Understanding groups and how they behave will be critical when we later discuss a strategy for change. The concept of a group entity will be expounded upon throughout this book since corruption itself is a group entity and not some individual or an organized conspiracy with a will to corrupt. Corruption is a collective byproduct of a social group.

Group vs Individual Interest

The fundamental premise of social change challenges the interest of the individual verses that of a group. This subject is fascinating and is a question of loyalty; perhaps there are ways to shape that loyalty.

Imagine we as a group live on a farm where we grow and eat food. If everyone works together, we can make a very large and productive farm. If we do not work efficiently, the farm is smaller than it could be. Some of us may be highly skilled and motivated farmers and produce more while others may have bigger appetites than others and eat more food. Appetites and contribution to the farm do not necessarily correlate. There may be other groups and other farms; and, we can examine the farm at various group levels. We can study a family farm, neighborhood farm, state farm, national farm or world farm. The larger the group, the more challenging it is to garner cooperation.

When we cooperate, we can maximize the size of the farm; share technology, resources and other good ideas to help other farms. We can work to our best ability and try to be as productive as possible. We can allocate food based on need or on productive merit. When we consider ourselves part of a larger group, we are driven to maximize the yield on the farm for everyone. Since we have nothing to hide, transparency should not be much of a problem. Karl Marx advocated that we should be as productive as possible and consume only according to our needs. However, human beings do not exactly work that way and Communism is a failed experiment. Human beings crave freedom and self-determination. Mandating cooperation is not genuine compassion and people resist infringement upon liberty. Organic compassion is far more lasting. History has shown that self-determination motivates and allocation of consumption by big brother is just plain terrible. Conversely, if we all think in terms of individual interests, we allow the strong to thrive and the weak to starve. Enough envy between the not-as-strong and the strong is an invitation for corruption.

When we corrupt, anything goes. We can sleep while others work. We can sneak in late at night to steal food and trample over edible produce in the process. We can force the group to take a few people out of production to act as late night security or as fence builders or locksmiths such that we do not maximize the yield potential of the farm. Sometimes some of us will starve while others stuff themselves. A surprisingly large number of workers are taken out of production when the honor system breaks down. After all, human beings are animals and animals are basically lazy, trying to consume the most with the least amount of effort and to corrupt if they can get away with it.

Consider two loyalties faced by the individual. (1) to act in the best interest of the group or (2) to act in the best interest of self. Those that act in the best interest of a group are less prone to corruption because there is no gain to the group. A group minded person sees the farm as a zero-sum game. Corruption is primarily motivated by individual gain. Some of us are naturally predisposed to be loyal to a group while others are predisposed towards loyalty to self. Corruption is crossing the line between adding genuine value and elbowing the guy next to you for personal gain.

Mandating a controlled society is in direct violation of the innate human desire to be free. It is better to encourage loyalty to the group to preserve liberty. Forcing equalization of consumption removes the motivation to work harder for more right to consume. How might we encourage ourselves to voluntarily think more in terms of group interest over personal interest? Reducing envy is a big step towards eliminating corruption (not confused with wealth redistribution).

We naturally gravitate towards like-minded people. We tend to be compassionate or at least empathetic to them. Cooperation on a family farm may be easier than on a neighborhood farm. When I work side by side with a disabled sister, I might work a little harder on her behalf because I know her, have affinity for her, and can empathize with her plight. She would likely be appreciative if she saw me work so she can eat. A faceless farmer in another county with the same disability would not be nearly as meaningful to me. If I happened to help them out in some way, I would just be a faceless Good Samaritan. If they met me on the street, I would still be a stranger and they would not have had the opportunity to see me sweat in the fields on their behalf. There is a word for this, *Propinquity*, which is the tendency to develop relationship with those we encounter frequently.

The solution is to create enough interaction to develop genuine empathy because it leads to unforced compassion. The more the strong and weak understand each other, the more empathy, compassion, trust, and appreciation they will share and less likely they will corrupt. More importantly, they lose the nimble ability to rationalize bad behavior because others in the group are no longer faceless. If people learned to think more in terms of group and less in terms of self, the farm just got a whole lot bigger.

To mandate equalization and force the strong to provide for the weak violates basic human liberty. Likewise, you can never force someone to think differently than they do. However, strongly encouraging interaction will naturally lead people to think beyond just themselves and part of something larger... hmm, like a group.

Imagine an almost mandatory 40hr annual community service program. Program participants pay an income tax 1% less than those who are not. A little freedom to opt out is preserved, but for all practical purposes, this strongly encourages participation. When people are actively involved in helping others, they organically gain empathy. That CEO helping a kid from the inner city with his homework might prompt the CEO and the kid to see each other differently. The handful of people, who cleaned up a park, might be less inclined to toss trash on the highway. They might even talk to each other and share life stories. Volunteers at the VA could help soldiers see that others care, inspiring them to move forward with their lives, providing the worker an appreciation for what it means to sacrifice a leg for the cause of freedom. The possibilities are limited only to imagination. The tiny incremental gains in understanding would slowly creep into the psyche of the nation and prompt us to think of ourselves as part of something bigger. This slow drip strategy encourages us to voluntarily shed self-interest in lieu of group interest. Instead of isolating ourselves in a microcosm of like-mindedness we expand who we are as a nation. Helping others creates happiness for all parties, especially for the person doing the giving.

The reasons for class divide and polarized views are that people do not really understand each other. People naturally create microcosms and surround themselves with like-minded people with similar lives. A little cross-pollenization is in order so that opposing sides simply understand what it is like to be in someone else's shoes. If this were to occur, I doubt liberals would institute Robin Hood laws so readily or that conservatives would maintain their simplistic views regarding the ease of economic mobility. Even social issues might be less polarized if an evangelical spent a day or two with a gay person or an executive spent time with a janitor. Longstanding myths are replaced with facts. It is an opportunity to close our mouths and open our ears.

D.   The Cosmic Ideology Premise

When discussing fair and unfair, right and wrong, or any other issues of morality, it is important to address the fundamental premises we might have with respect to the Cosmic Drama.   Who are we? Why are we here? Do we have purpose? Since we share this planet with others, is there some basic morality code that might determine what is okay and what is not okay? This fundamental view of the Cosmic Drama is the foundation that supports our most basic motivation for everything we do.

I really wanted to avoid the topic of religion since it triggers so many powerful emotions, however, like it or not, believer or not, religion has permeated our culture and in particular, Christianity. Christianity is on our currency and behind our debates; few politicians get elected who do not at least fake it or show deference to it. Christianity is the dominant religion in our American Culture and absolutely requires consideration.

An independent movement requires a soul and some moral beacon to follow for motivation. If such a movement is to have an agenda, it first needs principles.   Principles require some agreed upon universally acceptable set of values and values require some view of ourselves in relation to others.   My intention is to create enough common ground between believers and non-believers for a mutual purpose without slipping into a debate over divine truth. The goal is to identify common ground and to avoid divisive ideology. For Christians, well… you all know the story. I would like to invite non-Christians to consider the metaphorical truths of Christianity which do not require faith at all.

Consider Four Ideology components within Christianity.   The first component is Godology. Is there a God or, perhaps, how might we define God should we force ourselves to acknowledge one? Godology poses such questions as: How did we get here? Is there a purpose? What's it all about, if anything?

An interesting question to pose to agnostics might go like this. "For a moment accept that there is this word, "God". It can describe anything you like. It can be a noun, a verb, or an adjective. It can be an entity or just a concept. How would you define that word?" With such a liberty, we can all probably accept either God as a real entity or a conceptual metaphor. All of us have some Godology in our lives, even atheists. An atheist might say, I know there is creation caused by the Big Bang, we are here and we interact with others. There is love in the world I seem to have some spiritual connection to the world around me. If I force myself to define the word, God, that is it. Christians may vigorously disagree with the atheist but it is all forms of Godology.

The second ideology component is Jesusology. What did he say, what was his message and how does the message apply to our lives. Jesusology can be a divine axiom or a utilitarian view asking, does this make sense, would humanity be better off heeding the message; would we as individuals be better off? The general theme is represented by the Golden Rule, "Do unto others as you would have them do unto you." Be compassionate and go beyond ego; consider yourself to be part of something larger. Arguably, Jesusology is quite similar to Buddhism, namely compassion and altruism absent of any dogma. (Buddhist has no concept of Supreme Being and has no ideological dogma; faith is irrelevant as truth is an empirical experience). Again, the message is a general message shared by many other religions of the world. For the socially conscious, this is not a terribly difficult message to accept regardless of faith.

The third ideology I would call Christology. Is there life after death and how do we get to the good place? Is there a master plan whereby through Jesus the Christ we can get to that better place? Is there an absolute authority above us all that compels us to behave in a particular way, or else? Christology is not provable. It is a matter of faith. While the first two ideologies are not too difficult to accept, Christology separates the believer from the non-believer. Many will stop exploring Godology and Jesusology because they get hung up on Christology. In my view, it is like throwing the baby out with the bath water.

The final ideology component is Churchology, arguably started by Paul, the most influential and prolific author of the New Testament and a man who never knew Jesus, personally. Churchology is what man does with the first three ideologies. How does it all fit together, how do we read between the lines when no specifics are offered, and what are the rules.

Churchology is subject to the interpretations of others and is often frustrating. Some individual or group entity has the nerve to proclaim that he has got it all figured out and others should follow his interpretation. Some Churchology is good such as getting together occasionally to reflect on how we can be better people or maybe starting a project to help the poor. However, some Churchology acts on another agenda.

Many non-Christians have become frustrated with Churchology and see certain aspects as hypocritical or down-right evil. Groups based on ideology have a natural tendency to homogenize members towards the same ideology. Many do not like being stuffed into the homogenized box, and will not associate with churches since they dislike having some package crammed down their throats. Hard core Christian churches have a stunning ability to rationalize bad behavior and rely on the Almighty as the sole custodian of our planet.

When Sarah Palin proclaims, "Drill baby drill", I cannot help but think that something at the core of her ideology tells her that God has provided all the natural resources we need. To have the audacity to suggest God may have miscalculated the amount of oil he placed here on earth during Creation 7,000yrs ago would be an insult to the Almighty. Non-Creationists would argue that it takes 2 million years to cook up another batch of oil according to science. Oil is a precious resource that we cannot environmentally burn all at one time and is critical to our economy and national defense. We cannot just suck it out of the ground and burn it into the air as fast as we know how as if there is no tomorrow. Often behind the rhetoric of evangelicals is a premise that we are NOT the custodians of our society or of our environment. Instead, the world we live in is squarely in the hands of God; virtue is karma currency that you cash in at heaven's gate. In fact, take away the whole concept of heaven and hell and we might see life as far more precious and might be just a little more compassionate.

Would a suicide bomber strap a bomb to his chest if he believed in absolute death? Would we opt for more diplomacy and less armed conflict because soldiers are thinking twice about why they are killing and dying? When we pass a homeless battered woman on the street, could we rationalize walking by her thinking, "Hang in their honey, life is short and heaven is eternal? You will be okay if you just stay right by God." Or, would we realize that if we do not help, no one else will and she will suffer her one and only existence? Take away heaven and life is even more precious. Religion can be both a positive and negative for social good if we do not pervert the message with rationalizations. Perhaps we might realize that we have been blessed with our beautiful precious planet and we are all here together to make whatever world we choose to have.

As wonderfully described by Reza Aslan, **Jesus was a corruption crusader**. Believer or not, this is a fact difficult to dispute although believers might attach a different motivation. Jesus spends a good amount of time with John the Baptist and a group called the Essenes, who taught communality, brotherly love, and ritualistic water cleansings outside the Jewish authority that was highly corrupt at the time. Jesus was a Galilean, an area known for rebellion to both Rome and to those who served Rome. The time was hot and the enslavement felt by the citizens towards Rome was at a boiling point. Jesus gains many followers and for many reasons. He has a new vision for how the world should be that is revolutionary for its time and revolutionary for all time, from Gyork to the present. At the time, the temple was a toll gate to God and a money machine for both Rome and the Jewish leadership. Jesus challenged it and was killed for it.

The money machine is best described with this example.

If a rich or poor man had leprosy, he was considered to be on the wrong side of God because of something he did or some sin committed by his ancestors. Since leprosy was such a terrible scourge, the sin must have been pretty serious and would require a hefty blood sacrifice as prescribed in Leviticus. The sacrifice required two male lambs, one female lamb, a dove, some grain and a dash of oil. Now, only the high priest was authorized to perform a bona fide sacrifice, so here is what had to happen.

Since the man was "unclean", he could not enter the temple grounds. Instead, an agent of the temple would negotiate the sacrifice on his behalf. First toll was a fee for the ritualistic bath required outside the temple, then the temple tax equal to about two days' wages. Now the currency outside the temple was the Roman denarii and transactions within the temple had to be in shekels, so next stop is the money changers who extracted another fee. Cha-ching-bada-bing! The animals could not be just any ordinary animal off the range. They had to be raised for the specific purpose of ritual sacrifice and the temple had the goods. Since there was considerable expense in ridding this sin, the leper surely would not want to take any chances with generic sheep, so he paid up. Finally, the high priest sacrificed the guts of the animal and kept the usable parts for the last bit of profit. The priest never guaranteed a cure, that was up to God. The sacrifice only atoned for the sin. While this went on 24 hours a day, one might wonder how many sheep got recycled through a back door to another leper. Mess with the money machine and you are asking for big trouble from the profiteers.

*Crucifixion was reserved for sedition and seditionists were called "robbers". Crucifixion was a public statement not to mess with Rome's coffers. Jesus marches into Jerusalem with his message during Passover, in which estimates say the city swelled to over a million people. Tensions were high and the Romans were understaffed. The climax of his story is when Jesus upends the tables of the money changers and scatters those selling sacrificial goods. He has an opportunity to get away but sticks to the cause to see it through to the tragic end like a true hero, forever making a difference. While the rest is debatable by honest people, **Jesus was definitely an anti-corruption crusader**.*

The protestant reformation against the Catholic Church was a later reaffirmation of this theme. While I love the Catholic Church, and find myself at mass most Sundays, the Church has sins of its own. At the time, the Church was another toll gate to God. To be right by God, a believer needed a priest; only a priest could intercede on a believer's behalf with the system of sacraments and indulgences. The high clergy pretty much had whatever they wanted; and, in fact the celibacy of priests can be traced back to the church not wanting heirs to large fortunes. Martin Luther was a corruption crusader who broke down the toll booth and suggested a direct dialogue between God and man.

We might unite, despite our diversity of backgrounds, around a common theme that the metaphors of Jesus' teachings have value and utility towards creating a better world. Advocating is not to the exclusion of other religious teachings, but since Christianity seems to be the dominant subtext of our culture for the time being, to rally around a general common theme of creating a non-corrupt and compassionate society for ourselves, makes sense. The key, however, is to employ a set of rules that target corruption correctly, since all rules impinge upon liberty. We must strike the right balance between anticorruption and liberty or else we will soon live in a police state. A great example comes from some homeowner's associations. The rules start off making sense. After all, who wants a neighbor raising chickens next door? But some HOA's morph into something unrecognizable, with overzealous board members who will walk up to your home with a color palette to check if your window blinds match one of the five preapproved colors. While we must create rules to limit corrupt power, we must also defend our liberties with equal zeal.

E.   The Harmony of the Road

Have you ever been a passenger in a car when the driver is barreling down the freeway and the chemistry just does not feel right? There is an overloaded semi swaying to the left, a huge truck on the right, and a sports car texting a friend about to change lanes. The driver continues on, seemingly oblivious, and comments, "If there is an accident, it won't be my fault." Meanwhile all you can think is, "Yeah numbskull, but we are in a projectile traveling 70 mph and could get squished like a bug." Who cares if you are right or wrong? There is a certain harmony of the road much like there is to life. In both cases, we all know some people that just do not seem to get it, although they very much think they do.

We cannot control everything in our lives; just about anything can happen at any time. Our crazy driver can drive this way for the rest of his life and never get hurt, while the safest driver in the world can get T-boned and killed by a drunk driver running a red light at 4am. The best we can do is create a cone of probability where good things are more likely to happen but the roll of the cosmic dice is still a factor. Recognizing the harmony of your environment and finding your place within that harmony widens the cone of probability that you will experience a positive outcome, lessening the risk of chance. The more we can incorporate consistency with natural, social, and cultural harmonics, the more successful and long lasting the results will be. The main question is at what group level in the hierarchy are we solving for. Some of us can only think in terms of just ourselves, like our crazy driver who thinks, *My lane, My right of way*. Others think in terms of higher levels of our group tree, like you, the vehicle passenger, "This car is in harmonic cooperation with the group of cars that surround me. What each of us do individually and how we all adjust to the circumstance will determine if the harmony is maintained."

When trying to improve political issues, we must look for solutions that are in harmony with our nature as human beings and within our culture lest we create cacophonic discord that is in conflict. We live in an interrelated social ecosystem whereby positive change in one area may cause negative consequences somewhere else in the ecosystem. For example, we can raise the minimum wage to $30/hour which to some may sound like a great idea, especially to the guy making $9/hour, but it is in dis-harmony with the free market and might have negative consequences. The guy currently making $9/hour will probably be unemployed. There is a harmonic balance to be struck or else it will likely fail.

*At 16, my good son lost his motivation for school and was about to give up. He rebelled in the ways a 16yr old can. I had to explain to him that when he turned 18, he would either be living in a dorm at college or be flipping hamburgers while sharing a crappy apartment downtown. He no longer would be living at home. Our discussion was painful as I told him that if it meant living under a bridge, so be it! It was especially hard for me as I was fully prepared to follow through and watch him hit rock bottom. I have learned that **you can never help someone who does not participate in the solution**. I had to show him a clear picture so would have no illusions that portrayed an unrealistic harmony between his apathy and what he wanted in the real world. It was not easy, especially as tears welled in his eyes. My heart wanted to write him checks for the rest of his life, but had I done so, I may as well have handed him a rope and chair because I would have implicitly told him that I did not believe in him and destroyed his self-esteem. As it turned out, he was mighty upset with me but turned his grades around and now lives in a dorm.*

We focus too much on solving social issues in isolation and often fail to consider the ramifications. Harmony is best observed at a distance; like a choirmaster, we must step back to hear all the voices. After all, it is the blend of voices that the audience will hear.

An independent movement has the best chance of success if its objectives are in harmony with the social ecosystem, the nature of human beings and our culture as Americans. Since our social ecosystem is so interrelated, one can never expect perfection. Rather, like an exercise in linear programming, there is a best fit solution, similar to turning a series of knobs to optimize the best possible outcome.

Solutions are not always intuitive. Sometimes the exact opposite prescription turns out to be a better course of action. **The less encumbered we are by ideology; the freer we are to explore alternatives**. Here is what my daughter taught me.

When my kids were in grade school, my daughter was frustrated with a mean kid who would put her down verbally. My daughter's intuition was to have a better "comeback" line to win the verbal sparring contest. She had seen other kids do it with some success and wanted some dad advice to provide her with a little ammo. My daughter's intuition was to one up her competition. With an ideology that gave her an overdeveloped sense of fairness, equalizing the playing field matched her sensibilities. We had fun coming up with some clever comebacks that brought out the juvenile in me. I could see right away that the comebacks were inconsistent with my daughter's gentle nature and clearly unharmonious. So, I asked the question, "What would be the opposite course of action; and that does not mean to do nothing?" The first answer we came up with was to superlatively complement the bully. When the bully criticized the quirky gait of her walk, she would reply that the bully was the clearly the best walker in the class and would appreciate lessons. Although it was a bad idea, it defined the spectrum of possibilities and got my daughter out of her ideology of fairness through one-upmanship. We then studied why this corruptor bully criticized her and agreed that it was about power. She bullied because she could control the emotions of another human being and the power made her feel good. The more emotion she could invoke, the better she felt.

We played with a number of ideas and decided that when the bully started to criticize her, she would yawn and ask the bully to repeat herself because she did not quite hear. Then, with a stone face showing no emotion, ask yet another time to hear it again. If criticism continued, she would ask the bully to wait while she took her time rummaging for a piece of paper; ask the bully to please write it down so she can remember, hand the bully the paper; and then, immediately walk away.

The solution worked faster than I could have hoped and by the second day it was over. The point is that the solution was the polar opposite of her intuitive strategy and worked because it was within my daughter's nature to execute. It got her out of her ideology of fairness, to study the problem from a distance. The strategy was a head shot to the real issue - to remove the power gratification of the bully.

F.   IQ and EQ

We come into this world with several variables that set us apart. First, our brains are all wired differently. We have different IQs and EQs. Most know about IQ so let me explain EQ or Emotional Quotient. EQ is one's ability to sacrifice in the short term for a greater future good. EQ is most easily explained in this simple test given to children. A child is given his or her favorite doughnut and told that they are free to eat the doughnut, but if they wait 20 minutes they will get to enjoy two doughnuts. The tester leaves and the cameras watch. The kid with the high EQ will hold out for the second doughnut. The kid with the low EQ may ponder the situation for a few minutes (some just seconds) and then scarf the doughnut, forgoing the extra doughnut. Low EQ is often associated with Attention Deficit Disorder (ADD).

After Gyork was banished for stealing cave girls, he moved from a hunting community to a farming community. The whole psyche of the community was different. ADD was a valuable asset to the hunters. Those with ADD were risk takers and instead of focusing well on just one thing at a time, they focused on many things (perhaps not so well) all at once. Hunting required either bravery or at least some disregard for risk. Hunting also required multi-sensory processing. If a hunter could not multitask, he would not notice all the subtle information necessary to coordinate with the hunting party and probably would not eat that night. Game was not always available and the hunters hunted whenever they could. When game was scarce, they just had to try harder, traveling further away and taking more risks.

In the new farming community, Gyork had to learn very different skills. The farmers had a better sense of time and consequence as they had to plan more. The process of farming required tilling the field, planting the seed at just the right time, and watering them regularly. It required discipline, patience and focus. There was far better food management and the farmers had a developed food storage system to sustain themselves during winter months. Gyork lost his propensity to steal women as the population of the farming community was far greater for a given slice of earth. Neander farm girls seemed to be everywhere and Gyork had learned patience in his new community.

Gyork found that farming was easier and less risky than hunting. He noticed that the community had much more available time to study the stars and create fancy tools and weapons. Occasionally, when the hunting villages ran out of food or women, they would band together and wage war against his new farming community. Although the hunters had courage, they were no match for the farmers who could muster a larger well-organized army and had fancy weapons to defend themselves. Gyork was conflicted as on one skirmish he had killed one of his old hunting cave dwelling brothers. That night, Gyork told a story to the children around the fire to express his deep sadness. The story was about two brothers who made sacrifices to the sun god. One was a hunter and the other a farmer. The farmer was jealous that the sun god found more favor with the hunter's animal sacrifice. One day he killed his brother and was banished with a mark of shame. After telling the story, Gyork began to weep sorrowfully and left the fire inconsolable.

To some extent we can compensate for IQ by working harder. EQ is a different animal and seemingly harder to change although possible to some extent. Group time is understandably much slower than Individual time since it takes time to gain consensus. **Many group entities tend to have low EQ's.** Groups with low EQ's often have a disproportionately powerful member or subgroup with ambitions that are misaligned with the group as a whole. The leadership within a group has disproportionate influence within the group and can hijack the will of the group. Groups need to run at slow time to gain consensus. Leaders within a group run off faster clocks and can get the group to act impulsively. The internal conflict of interests causes the group to behave erratically as the power base uses the group for personal gain.

The EQ of today's political body is very low as it is with the voting public who elects them. The dynamics of politicians within a group is very interesting. Think of a particular political party either Democrat or Republican. The utility of the group is the strength in numbers both in voting alliances and election alliances. The Party has a platform that seems to represent most views of its politician members. There are also subgroups within each party as well as caucuses such as the Freedom Caucus and the Black Caucus for which these subgroups will support each other on certain issues. The party leadership is a group of veteran politicians that bully with rank as well as the freshmen politicians who are aligned as newbies trying to figure things out and survive politics.

Political groups are based on the utility that the group can help members to get elected and to help advance one another's agenda, sometimes based on principle but most importantly, to get re-elected. A political group affiliation is not entirely voluntary for politicians. You can be removed from the group involuntarily simply by losing the next election. Politicians automatically have a bifurcation of interests. First, they must survive re-election. Then and only then, can they participate as members of their respective party. Losing an election is death to a politician. From a politician's point of view, what is the point of advancing the party agenda if you are kicked out by the voter tantamount to being a dead politician? In the doughnut experiment described earlier for kids, the time frame was 20 minutes. For the politician, the EQ timeframe is the next election which explains why we see politicians campaign differently in primaries than they do in the general election. The elections need to be won in sequential order and is one reason why the House of Representatives (re-elected every 2 years) has a different EQ dynamic than the Senate (every 6 years).

With such an unstable alignment of interest, no wonder political groups have such a low EQ. This alone is a great argument for term limits from the perspective of group dynamics. With term limits, the politician does not wonder whether he will get whacked or not; he already knows he is going to get whacked. With that out of the way, he can focus on his principles. The group power is diminished and its EQ makes a quantum leap. Now the group can focus on a principled agenda. Why is this important? Remember that low EQ seeks short term gratification at the expense of maximizing long term benefit through principled legislation. The low EQ of political groups is why Washington does not behave rationally and is why Social Security is insolvent. Everyone knows it and we have known it for a very long time, but no Congress has been able to fix the problem because the short-term pain is death to most politicians.

Clearly politicians will resist term limits. After all, who would ever choose certain death? This is where a particular strategy fits and there is a concrete example where it did. Prior to a legislation change in the 90's, if a politician did not use his campaign funds, he was able to keep them when he retired. This was a perfect prescription for legalized graft. Contributions to a campaign war chest meant that either the politician could decide to use it for re-election or to retire and buy a home in Aspen, CO. When I heard this was ever legal, my jaw hit the floor, and hard. Somehow, the revelation got a lot of public attention and pressure was on Congress to change the law but no one in Congress wanted to give up their grafted treasure chest. The bill was blocked from ever reaching the floor for a vote. The only way it got passed was to "grandfather" existing politicians exempting them - a way of saying "Okay, but from now on." The provision was certainly a chicken s#&t way to do politics but at least it got done.

The strategy is to separate the politician's personal interest from his duty as a rational legislator by forward dating laws. This strategy is still a cowardly way to do politics but it pays to be pragmatic when you need to get something important done in the face of low EQ obstructionists. In the case of laws to change term limits, forward date the change such that politicians do not see it as personally threatening, say starting 12 years from now. Doing so is a way of saying, "From now on" and has the best chance of success without getting bogged down with it being fair or unfair. The more you get the American mind to move towards a stronger EQ, the empirical progress will encourage more. The best place to start is to improve the EQ of politicians who make the rules.

G.   The Morality of Equalization

There is no point in trying to make everyone equal in ability since it is virtually impossible and it would bring up another major morality point. Recall the metaphor that corruption is like a foot race where one person elbows his opponent so that he can win at the other's expense and imposed disadvantage. But if one opponent is naturally faster than another, is he obliged to disadvantage himself by wearing sandbags so that the other has an equal chance at winning? Hmm... interesting, but no. We all have the right to life, liberty, and the pursuit of happiness. Those that are more able will naturally have a higher expectation on themselves. In addition, as contributors to society, working at the level of the lowest common denominator does no one any good. To equal the playing field may be chivalrous, but doing your best with the gifts you have at no forced disadvantage to another, is all I would argue is required. Compassion must be encouraged through other clever means and can be achieved; forced compassion is a recipe for resentment.

H.   A Few Behavior Lessons

History has taught us several important lessons that we seem to almost habitually repeat, either because we do not remember or because the action required to prevent mistakes from the past is somehow contrary to our nature. Quite often, allowing our emotional instincts to supersede our intellectual rationale stands in our way. We may have all the IQ in the world but with a low EQ, we lack patience and act impulsively. Groups seem to naturally have lower EQ's that are harder to control requiring exceptional leadership.

The ideas below will help explain how corruptors corrupt. This handful of ideas will also establish a foundation for later strategies and tactics.

Fear is Life's Most Powerful Motivator

Self-preservation is perhaps our most fundamental motivator, as it is for any species. Fear is a necessary requirement for survival; it should be no surprise that we humans have a highly-developed capacity for fear of anything that threatens our sense of security. We act when we perceive a threat whether it be real or imagined. Fear triggers the amygdala, a part of the primitive brain entirely separate from our frontal lobe, that processes rational thought. Fear of what might happen is more powerful than the actual outcome. Our imagination can conjure up all sorts of horrible scenarios and the primitive brain is not always rational. Remember the fears you had as a child that, once experienced, turned out to not be such a big deal. I recall being terribly afraid of being punched in the nose until it happened. Fear triggers either fight to destroy or flight to avoid. Fear is a far stronger motivator than opportunistic drives such as greed.

When I was a derivatives salesman at Lehman Brothers, we were sent to Vermont on a sales retreat. The take away was that the biggest motivator for action was fear. We were given a five-step process for fear based sales:

5 Steps for fear-based persuasion:

1. Identify a problem
2. Impart the seriousness of the problem by emphasizing consequences
3. Impart urgency to fix the problem
4. Dispel the arguments of the nay-sayers
5. Lead the poor victim out of his dilemma as the "Rain Maker"

In bond sales it might go like this:

1. Your portfolio is out of balance
2. If you do not beat the index or are out of line with your peers, what will your performance look like or your ability to raise more money?
3. Markets change quickly, you'd better fix this quick or your job is at risk.
4. Do not listen to the other analyst or those thoughts in your head, stay safe.
5. Here's a solution, I have what you need, let's do it now.

On Fundamentalist Christian radio (I have actually heard this):

1. Ever wonder what happens when you die?
2. Do not you want to see your family when you die? Hell is a bad place.
3. You never know when it could happen, Tomorrow? In a month? When?
4. The devil is telling you otherwise through evil people he has won over.
5. Get on the bus. Stop thinking. We'll drive. We have got it all figured out.

Creating fear in others will cause them either to yield to our will, fight us, or temporarily yield to our will long enough to regroup to return with a more formidable opposition. Fear is not to be confused with respect. Respect has nothing to do with fear. Respect is an entirely different tool for getting others to comply with our will. Respect is earned while fear through intimidation is imposed. Creating fear intimidates behavior if the consequences of not complying are unacceptable. But unless the fear subsides, it only creates a motivation to alleviate the fear. Creating fear in others naturally creates fear in ourselves since we can never be certain that they would not find an opportunity to retaliate. To walk around the neighborhood with a big club to intimidate others requires that you continually walk the neighborhood with a club in your hand. Mobsters are paranoid intimidators. Fear alone is a bad instrument of any policy domestic or foreign though it has been used precisely as an instrument of policy.

When we are in a state of fear, it is in our interest to gather more information to first determine if there is a legitimate threat or only a perceived threat. Fear motivates action, but not all actions are in our best interest. We need to distinctly transfer command and control from our primitive brain to our frontal cortex where we can make rational decisions that are in our best interest.

When we have put others in a state of fearing us, we must lead them out of their state of fear, otherwise they will remain unpredictable and dangerous. The only logical alternative is to destroy them which is barbaric. To reason with someone who fears you is difficult as they are stuck in their primitive brain.

Millions of examples exist of how fear has been a bad motivator to get humans to do very bad things. Domestically, white fear of blacks was largely responsible for Jim Crowe laws. Look around the globe and you will see that most world conflict is based on fear. Democracies are fearful of totalitarian regimes and totalitarian regimes are afraid of everyone, especially their own citizens. Corrupt institutions are naturally fearful since they themselves do not want to be treated as they treat others. They lack moral authority precisely for this reason and cannot influence the behavior of others through respect. Instead, they must intimidate, and deceive. When the United States allows personal interest to supersede principle, they too are treating others differently than how they expect to be treated, and we are put in an indefensible position that undermines our moral authority and our influence. In such cases, we can either correct our bad behavior or we must continue to intimidate. Influence via respect is a far more sustainable than through intimidation.

Never Give Someone Nothing to Lose

Desperate people are dangerous because they feel they have nothing to lose. Influencing someone in such a state of desperation is very hard because consequences mean nothing to them. A starving man will be more prone to steal food than if he were not hungry. An army defending their homeland will fight more vigorously than the occupying army because they have everything to lose. This was probably the biggest blunder of the second Gulf War. Paul Bremmer disbanded the Iraqi army removing their means to support their families; fired all the Baathists that knew how to run the infrastructure of the country with no means of income; and installed a Shiite government who further disenfranchised the Sunni population from the political process. Was it any wonder why al Qaida and ISIS found support from the disenfranchised unemployed Sunnis who now had nothing to lose? To put someone in a desperate state means that they will always fight you. You have three choices. You can endure the fighting, destroy them, or lead them out of their desperation so that they have something worth preserving.

A Loss Hurt's More Than a Gain Helps

In economic terms avoiding a loss is no different than enjoying a gain, however in our psyche there is a big perceived difference. Think of this scenario. How would you feel if someone took away half your wealth? Now ask yourself how you might feel if someone were to give you an amount equal to half your wealth? The pain of loss has more emotional charge than the pleasure of gain.

Happiness Is An Expectation

In our culture, happiness is the expectation that things will improve in the future. The greater the change and the sooner the improvement, the more intense is our sensation of happiness. The intensity of anxiety is the counterpart. Consider winning the lottery. You think of all the ways that your life will improve and you are happy. But many lottery lives turn tragic as most people do not know how to assimilate such a rapid change. For most, this is the peak of their wealth curve. Once they have assimilated their new situation, there is no more expectation of an improvement from the money alone. Unless they can continually create an expectation that their lives will improve, the happiness from winning the lottery will soon wane.

People are happy when they have hope for a better tomorrow. The hope could be a new experience, a fitter body, a safer environment, something to be learned, better prospects for your children, or something purchased. Anything positive to look forward to, will create a general feeling of happiness. Hope is the realistic expectation that there are possibilities. People without hope have little to lose.

Lack of Patience

We want what we want and we want it now. It is the low EQ of a large group. With the internet, information flows at lightning speed. Take any major news event and you will find CNN voraciously trying to get facts out to the public. When facts are unavailable, all the possibilities are hashed over and over until the facts are known. Reporters pepper officials for answers when information is still inconclusive. The words, "I do not know, yet" while perfectly reasonable, are just not acceptable to the media, or seemingly to the public. Well vetted reliable information that takes time is far more valuable than incomplete speculative information. With impartial information, we fill in the gaps with past patterns that are often driven by fear. Reaching for immediate answers is natural for us, although acting on incomplete answers can be dangerous.

Revenge

Humans have a very strong sense of justice. Everyone likes to see the villain get it in the end. Such a strong emotion is a mandatory element in any American movie. However, there are times when revenge is not in our best interest. Nelson Mandela had plenty reason to seek revenge against the White Afrikaans who had abused their minority power with the policy of Apartheid. The Apartheid government even enslaved Mandela unjustly for almost 30 years. He brilliantly realized it was not in his interest to seek revenge. Despite being fully deserving of retribution,

Mandela in his wisdom, recognized the usefulness of the white minority as keepers of the infrastructure and necessary economic participants. He set up a committee for truth and reconciliation but never sought revenge. It was not in his interest nor was it in the interest of the black South Africans to do so.

Cuban Americans displaced during the Castro regime and who lost all their wealth are still furious with the Castro government and many are against any relationship with Cuba. Isolation has not worked to end the Castro regime and re-engagement would likely do more to ending the power of the regime and help both Americans and Cubans.

Those out for revenge are thought to be dangerous and dangerous people should be feared. People who are afraid of those seeking revenge are dangerous, themselves. World War II was in part caused by the French insisting on revenge after World War I in the Treaty of Versailles. Although doing so felt good, it was not in anyone's interest to humiliate Germany with impossible war reparations. That lesson taught us to handle postwar Germany and Japan very differently following WWII and the outcome proved fruitful.

Envy

Frans de Waal on a TED Talk described a video experiment using monkeys. These monkeys would perform a task and receive a cucumber as a reward. The monkeys were quite satisfied with the cucumber treat and would perform the task repeatedly. However, to a monkey, a grape is a far more desirable treat. When one monkey saw he was receiving a cucumber and the other monkey a grape for the same task, he stopped doing the task and got quite angry. In a short amount of time, the monkey was so mad it began throwing the cucumbers back at the experimenter.

Envy is a powerful motivator. When my father described the Depression as a happy time despite eating frogs and beans and wearing resewn clothes, I was surprised. The fact is that everyone in their social circle was in the same boat and it was far easier to endure the hardships. When I taught high school, kids from the swanky part of town could get quite put out if daddy did not buy as nice a car as the other daddies did. The school was a mixed class Catholic school and kids from the other side of town would be thrilled to have bus fare. We have a tendency to view our lot in life not in absolute but in relative terms. Envy is a powerful motivator to corrupt. When something others have is unattainable, we rationalize why we should have the same. The threshold to corrupt is lowered by envy.

Security & Liberty

People will give up their liberties when they feel that their security is at risk. Remember that fear is the greatest motivator of man. When the citizenry feels that their security is threatened, they will cede liberty to their leaders and give them broad powers to make the risk go away. The scenario has been repeated over and over again in history. From the Salem Witch hunts to Japanese internment camps to McCarthyism, we were more than willing to yield our civil liberties just to make the threat go away. I do not want to get into the argument as to whether the loss of liberty is legitimized by threats such as war or terrorism. What is important is that we are prone to ceding liberty in these environments and need to be vigilant. Fear is often deliberately used to manufacture or exaggerate threats to fit an agenda, providing an argument for fact checking and accurate risk assessment.

The Psychology of Corruption

Dr. Dan Ariely is a behavioral economist who performs clinical research to study corruption. He is a gifted speaker with an amazing story and passionately explores this topic. I had the good fortune to meet him at a conference. Dan posed the following scenario:

Ten people are in a room and each given $100. They may keep the $100 or may anonymously place it in a jar. At the end of the day, the money in the jar is multiplied by two and redistributed evenly to ALL 10 people.

If all ten people choose to put the money in the jar, then $1,000 goes into the jar, is multiplied by two and then $2,000 is redistributed such that *everyone receives $200 at the end of the day. But what if one person cheats and decides not to place his money in the jar? $900 goes into the jar. $1,800 is distributed to all ten and everyone receives $180 except the cheater who receives both the $180 and the $100 in his pocket (because he withheld it from the jar), or $280.*

Although no one knows who the cheater is, all ten people will have enough evidence to know that someone cheated. On the next round, more people will feel justified to cheat, shrinking the payout pie even further. In this example, the cheater has allowed his individual preference to supersede what is in the best interest of the group. He shrank the group pie so that he could wrangle a fatter slice. Doing so was easy since he could do it anonymously and there was no punishment. Members perceive a disloyalty to the group by others and feel less obligated to be loyal to a group with disloyal members. If you work out the math, cheating until there are five cheaters and five loyals is in everyone's individual interest. But, consider what happens at this equilibrium of cheating incentive. The overall benefit to the group is lessened. Would there ever be a circumstance when there would be more than five cheaters when it is not even to the advantage of the cheaters? The answer is sometimes. People will cheat not only for their personal advantage, they will cheat in retribution to the other cheaters and knowingly suffer themselves in the process.

Consider three components of cheating. What are the benefits, what are the consequences and what is the likelihood of suffering those consequences? This is a big point when studying corruption.

What would stop the corruption in this game? Transparency is one way. If everyone knew who was loyal and who was cheating, the cheating would lessen for many reasons. People could adjust their behavior based on whom and how many are cheating eliminating the advantage to cheat, and there is now a social consequence to cheating or peer pressure to be loyal.

How do you get people to act in the best interest of the group when individual interests shrink the pie? How does a group get a cheater to become a loyal? Does the group even have the right to force someone not to act in their best personal interest? That is an existential question, but in the end, it does not matter; the powerful set the rules. The group is free to decide the rules and others must abide by them or suffer the consequences. The group needs to decide what world they want to live in.

In Dr. Ariely's book, *Cheating and Deception*, he explains several reasons why people have a propensity to cheat. The solution lies in established rules, consequence and transparency. Many consequence tools are available, if we understand why people corrupt.   Many of the tools may be counterintuitive. For example, tests show that an atheist is less likely to lie when they swear on a Bible. Capital punishment (the ultimate consequence) has not proven to be a deterrent to capital crime. People will cheat less when they see those suffering the consequences as similar to themselves. People who are periodically reminded not to cheat will cheat less.

I happen to think that a continuum of archetypes exists where some of us naturally think in terms of individual interests and others think in terms of group interest and could be nature or nurture. Perhaps social education would encourage us to think in terms of group interest with regards to corruption.

In addition, what can we do as a society to have better empathy and loyalty to the group? Time for a social mixer, don't you think? What if we had a highly-encouraged community service obligation of 40 hours per year? Those that participate get a 1% tax credit. To maintain liberty, people can opt out and forego the tax credit. It is a way to gain mutual understanding across our many differences so that we become more empathetic and recognize the consequence corruption has on others. Interaction leads to communication → understanding → empathy → less fear, and hopefully, → compassion.

Corruption is Contagious

The rule of law is a critical concept. Once the rule of law is broken with impunity, there is no rule of law. **We as humans have an incredible ability to rationalize bad behavior especially when we have company.**

When we see friends and family cheat on taxes and get away with it, we can rationalize that if everyone else is doing it then why should not I be able to do it. At this point, the rule of law breaks down. No one wants to follow rules that others get away with, leading to phrases like "work the system". Seemingly, if you can get away with it then it must be okay, one reason why deep enforcement is so important for shaping the public mindset. Small infractions lead to big infractions.

Once the veil of corruption is pierced, further corruption becomes psychologically easier. All of us have exercised some form of corruption, either by downloading a pirated song or tossing a gum wrapper out the car window. Some have suggested a "reset button" whereby we agree upon a date and say from now on we will be good citizens and stop corrupt behavior. Dr. Dan Ariely has found that a reset button is very important for the success of a social campaign, as it psychologically reorients the perception that we all have a second chance. We have a new chance at psychological purity for past sins and it will be harder to pierce a new veil. Periodic metrics showing how we are doing will be good feedback. Exposing corruptors and reminders that we all belong to something larger, with a responsibility to be honorable citizens are also important.

Overlooking Minor Offenses

When people steal a lot from a few people, we take notice. When people steal a little from a lot of people, we look the other way. We do not enforce minor offenses. Some clever credit card scams will charge $0.99 to the cards of many people for two reasons. First, the charge is likely to be overlooked or blend in with common internet charges like an iTunes App charge. Second, for many people, to challenge the charge by calling the credit card company is not worth the 20 minutes. Corruption can be considered some form of theft. Over time, these minor thefts begin to add up to significant dollars. Enforcing minor offenses is important because we have to stick with universal principles and enforce all rules. Looking the other way on minor theft misses an opportunity to shape the mindset of the population towards correct behavior. We need to be consistent if we are going to change the mindset.

Crusaders are seldom rewarded for what they do on behalf of a group. So much of our apathy and unwillingness to improve is based upon this principle. Simply stating to someone (and nothing else) that it is not okay to cut in line or to toss a cigarette out a car window is a critical step to shaping the mindset as an empowered group. You do not need to enforce anything; you just need to say it is not okay. Think about what that does to the mindset of the nation.

Overlooking Major Offenses

If ever there was a major offense that no one really did anything about, it was the financial crash of 2008. Having spent 19 years on Wall Street myself in mortgage backed securities and derivatives, I can tell you that the culture of Wall Street is accurately described in Michael Lewis book, *The Big Short* . The take away was classic low EQ of a group. When there is money to be made, Wall Street will stretch the boundaries of logic to make a quick buck. There used to be what we called *The Eternal Put Option*, where big fat bonuses were one outcome and the worse that seemed to happen was that someone lost their job and went to work for another firm, often for more money. Wall Street group culture dominated anyone's individual sensibilities; the contagion of the money culture was overwhelming. The goal was to make as much money and as fast as you possibly could since tomorrow had no guarantees. Decisions were made on the spot, without bureaucracy by managers with a surprising lack of appreciation for risk. When there was money to be made, people checked their morality at the front desk and howled at the full moon.

No one wanted to fix the broken system because it cranked out so much money. No one knew where to start because it was such a mass conspiracy of fraud including traders, salesmen, rating agencies, regulators, and the political system all paid to play along. There was a gross indifference to the truth and few saw that the king had no clothes.

While I had left Wall Street 8 years before the 2008 crash, I saw the shady transactions my peers were making always finding some loop hole to exploit. In my day, the scam de jour were the bonds sold to the likes of Orange County. Cash accounts were to be low risk accounts with very little price risk. The regulations allowed for only AAA securities with maturities less than 1 year or government bonds less with maturities less than 3 years. The loop hole was that The Federal Home Loan Bank (FHLB) was a government bond and there was no regulation on how the rate of return was determined. The regulators simply applied the wrong rules that they felt would keep these bonds safe based only on what was currently available in the market place.

I covered the Atlanta FHLB that would do a riskless trade to receive cheap funding. Some client I did not know was sold a risky trade by another salesman. The investors were just plain stupid and greedy, enticed by the fat initial yields with embedded risk they did not understand. The trading desk would call me and ask if the FHLB would issue the risky bond and completely offset the risk with a derivatives contract that the trading desk had prepared. My customer was the FHLB that I was doing a service for by providing cheap financing. I did not know or care who was ultimately being duped into taking the risk by purchasing the risky bonds. It was not my job to know, yet I was blindly complicit and being rewarded for my complicity. I never questioned what was happening elsewhere in the firm. Orange County was not my customer. The FHLB never asked nor did they care. It was not their job to vet the customers of Lehman Brothers. Deep down, the FHLB and I both knew something was fishy, but since we benefited, we looked the other way. Legally, we did nothing wrong.

The risks on these bonds grew more and more obscene over time and eventually the market turned and they exploded creating $1.7BB in losses to a $7BB fund. When everyone finally realized just how risky these bonds were, the bonds were purchased back by Wall Street at a deep discount for even more profit, the derivatives underlying the bonds were unwound by the FHLB for profit to them as well and the bonds were retired. The winners were Wall Street and the FHLB. The stupid greedy investment managers simply lost their jobs. The real losers were the citizens of Orange County who depended upon regulators, money managers, and a financial system that would keep their money safe. This was a classic case of relying on specific regulation to limit the boundaries of corruption rather than conceptual regulation to attack the whole practice of financial corruption.

The 2008 crisis, despite having the benefit of experience of Wall Street excesses, dwarfed the crime of what was called the Orange County scandal (though Orange County was only one of many duped investors). The seed of the 2008 crisis began within 10 years of the Orange County scandal and had many times more impact.

When the 2008 crisis was over, one man went to jail, large bonuses were still paid, the tax payers assumed the loss, and although banks were too big to fail then, they are even bigger now that risks are ultimately borne by the public. Wall Street, even after receiving bailout money, spent tons of money on lobbying to make sure politicians left them alone. It has been only 9 years since the crisis and we put our heads in the sand going about our daily lives, thinking someone else has taken care of the problem when no one has. People have not rallied to do anything for several reasons. First, there are so many fingers pointing that no one knows where to start and the problem just seems too big. Second, it happened to a lot of us and we take comfort that we were not the only ones affected. When we have company as victims, we are not as mad. Trying to tackle Wall Street when politicians are paid to protect them is pointless. A corrupt entity is beating democracy through deception and confusion. The public can be depended upon to look the other way; after all, crusaders are seldom rewarded. We were mad, but not mad enough to make corruption a single-issue worth fighting above all other issues.

We still have not solved the problem. Why would Wall Street not try to exploit the system again when there seems to be no consequence? Just how many times will the pattern repeat until we cave dwellers band together with teeth, and say, enough?

Fortunately, in our political system, we have retained the power of the vote although no one yet has been able to rally an anticorruption movement with a single voice. Remarkably, the environment for such a voice is ripe for an independent voice to be heard over the din of corruption. We have the potential to break through the complacency we have been lulled into by a group dynamic that so far has been able to confuse, deceive, and demoralize.

III. Decorrupting American Politics

A.   A Word about SunTzu

Sun Tzu was a Chinese military strategist from around 500 BC who wrote *The Art of War*. His principles are still used today in war, business, and even life management. His principles have weathered the test of time as every major blunder in history can be attributed to some violation of Sun Tzu principles.

For those unfamiliar with Sun Tzu principles, I suggest you look them up sometime. Please do not confuse the military metaphors as anything but metaphor. For those familiar with Sun Tzu, you will quickly spot his principles embedded throughout the remainder of this book.

Here are a few of my paraphrased favorites:

- *Attack you enemy's strategy and then if necessary, his army*
- *Break the enemy's resistance without fighting*
- *Know thyself and know thy enemy*
- *Build your enemy a golden bridge [a way out] and lead him to it*
- *Always fight on a battlefield of your choosing*
- *Avoid a prolonged war*
- *All war is deception*
- *Attack with lightning speed and overwhelming force*
- *Divide your enemy's forces and attack where he is weakest*
- *Avoid recklessness, cowardice, temper, delicacy of honor, or over-solicitude*
- *Be harmonious with heaven, earth, moral purpose, method and discipline*

B.   Clear Objective

As a representative democracy, politicians make the rules in America. Presumably they are motivated by the will of the people, but we know that is barely true and not worth belaboring the point with examples.   True democracies work for very small groups but for a group of over 300MM people, a representative democracy is the only practical way to govern such a large nation.

The big disconnect in a representative democracy is that the rule makers also make rules for themselves, most importantly, how they are awarded the privilege of power.   The premise for awarding power is the premise of democracy, itself.   If you corrupt how power is awarded, then the democratic process and subsequent duties of governance will be corrupted.

Politicians need votes to be awarded power. [1] When voters feel that a candidate represents their wants and needs, the vote is cast. [2] The job of candidates is to convince voters, and; that is done by creating a perception that the candidate's interest is aligned with the voter. [3] The perception is created through communication, done predominantly by the media through TV, radio, and the internet. [4] To communicate that perception requires money that the politician generally does not have and must acquire through fund raising. [5] Fundraising is done by those who want something in return. [6]   Those with disproportionate wealth get disproportionate government representation.   Disproportionate representation, redefines democracy. [7]   Our rules for awarding power to politicians not only corrupt the election process, they also corrupt the legislative process and the behavior of all levels of government, a disproportionately large participant in commerce.

Steps to award power to politicians:

1.   Politicians need votes to be awarded power.
2.   Voters elect the candidate who represents their wants and needs.
3.   Candidates must create a perception that they represent wants and needs.
4.   The perception is communicated through the media.
5.   It takes money to communicate that perception through fund raising.

6. Fund raising is done by those who want something in return.

7. Disproportionate representation challenges the definition of democracy, itself.

Politicians make the rules for awarding power, as in the proverbial fox in the chicken coop. That politicians do not want the rules to change, should be no surprise. After all, they could successfully navigate these rules to get elected over any rivals. The individual politician is not necessarily to blame for corrupting our democracy; rather, the political group entity has corrupted our election process. Like any entity, this entity wants to survive and will resist change.

Fortunately, these series of steps define a battlefield in which the corrupted power entity (CPE) moves at will, plundering and pillaging the rest of us. The CPE is similar to an army that supports a malevolent monarch. Like any army, the CPE needs food, water, information, weapons and the like. It needs to cross bridges, build roads, and communicate. It is a group entity with a personality, ego, fears, values, hopes and dreams, supported by subgroups with traits of their own.

By identifying the series of steps and examining them in detail, it is possible to attack each step of the process in a concentrated effort to deprive the CPE of what it needs to survive to choke it OUT. Fortunately, the CPE entity has a very low EQ which is the worse quality of command, and each step in the corruption cycle is vulnerable. The attack must be swift, coordinated and overwhelming. The battle is just a formality and must be won by strategy before the fight ever takes place. The CPE is the ultimate source of all corruption in governance and to try to make real legislative progress before the CPE is either dead or neutered is pointless. To change the way schools are run or how we reform our tax code or any other economic, social, and foreign issue, you must first kill the source of corruption. This requires a "head shot" at the CPE.

Dismantling corruption can be done, but it will require building an army ourselves, with resources and a will to fight. No one will help in the fight unless they can be convinced that it is in their best interest to do so with a likelihood of victory. The better the plan, the easier the plan can be accomplished with the fewest resources. We have been beaten down and led to believe there is nothing we can do and that the CPE is too big and too powerful to beat. I am here to convince you that it has vulnerabilities and can be beat.

Clear Objective:

To enact laws at all levels of government that make our democracy truly representative by eliminating the behaviors that corrupt the election process, legislation, and the role of government as a participant in commerce. Then, to enact laws that protect against corruption within society.

The founding fathers never intended to have a truly representative democracy. The mindset at the time fully accepted a privileged class that had disproportionate representation. Natural leaders were from the elite aristocracy and natural followers were comprised of everybody else. Society would have to depend upon the benevolent wisdom of the ruling aristocracy to do what was in the best interest of all. Guess what happened when benevolence competed with the personal interest of the ruling aristocracy? Few founders ever considered the working class to have the capacity to think for itself. The concept of a pure representative democracy was redefined at the outset.

Many of us adhere to the concept of a free market; however, representation is not based on free market principles.

We hold these truths to be self-evident, that all men are created equal, that they are endowed by their Creator with certain unalienable Rights, that among these are Life, Liberty and the pursuit of Happiness.--That to secure these rights, Governments are instituted among Men, deriving their just powers from the consent of the governed.

When the currency of representation changed from one man-one-voice to a de facto one-dollar-one-voice, then free market principles with respect to governance, has been corrupted. We are simply using the wrong currency in governance.

We have made great improvements in governance corruption since the founding of our nation; however, the ill effects of past corruption have had a cumulative effect upon our nation, particularly in the last eighty years. It is more important than ever to make the correction and to make it now.

Corruption is not just at the federal level but is at all levels of government including state and local government. The objective focuses on all levels of government. While most of our attention and the attention of media is on federal government, state politics has far more impact on our day to day lives. Arguably, state and local politics deserves more of our attention. If a single state could develop an exemplary model of their own, it could be imitated by other states. A determined state might even convince the federal government to cede more control and budget to that state to address its own issues. Successful models and ideas are contagious.

Change requires new rules and new rules restrict the liberty of those benefiting from pay to play politics. Like the rules of the cave dwellers not to club men over the head for their women, some liberty will be lost. If others can't misbehave, then all are deprived of the freedom to misbehave.

C.   Creating an Independent Movement

1.   Politicians need votes to be awarded power.

American politics have traditionally been binary. On the right are the Republicans and on the left the Democrats. The groups are formed based on ideologies of conservatism and liberalism. Other parties have tried to enter the mix but they either became a subgroup of one of the binary parties or was too ineffective to matter.

The parties offer the utility of cohesiveness to its member politicians. A growing rift has formed within each party, forming subgroups of centrists and hardliners. Challenges have been made to the binary system of politics but most have failed and in fact only hurt the next most closely aligned party.

The best example occurred in the 1988 presidential election with what is now known as the *Ross Perot Effect*. Ross Perot, while most aligned with the right than the left, entered the race as an independent only to steal votes away from his most aligned rival, George H.W. Bush.   Perot's entrance as an Independent only helped the least aligned, Bill Clinton, get elected.   The 2000 election was a much closer election that created the term, *hanging chad*. The election was so close that Ralph Nader from the small Green Party made all the difference by only harming Al Gore. Nader was most similar to Gore and tilted the balance to George W. Bush.

The third party president is a bad option for now and we must not be seduced into thinking that a defined Independent Party is a goal in the foreseeable future, despite the fact that the majority of Americans consider themselves to be Independents (42%). What is far more effective is a unified Independent Movement. Initially, we should focus on Congress. A center movement is the only way to influence the rule makers to change the rules on how they are awarded power so that they are obliged only to their constituents and not to the "king makers" of special interest. The CPE is the head of the snake and until the CPE is destroyed, you cannot expect real change in governance.

Since the 2000 race, elections are won by the thinnest of margins. I believe that the close margins are indicative of general dissatisfaction since the marginal voter turnout is motivated by the "No Vote". An independent movement could wield some real power in the middle, especially with a low EQ political body.

Independents need a platform to rally around. Currently, they are not unified and are just swing voters with individual pet issues uncommitted to either party or their ideologies. While there can certainly be future agenda items, attacking prioritized issues one at a time is always best. **The very first platform issue needs to be a single-issue platform to rid governance of the CPE.**

The Independent Movement's primary mission would be to elect the candidate who will most likely support election reform to stop the systematic corruption in governance. If neither candidate supports election reform, always vote OUT the incumbent who has proven to support the CPE. It is important to focus on a universally accepted principle and not to get side tracked on other more divisive issues. The NRA uses this highly effective strategy that should be imitated. Forget for a moment whether you agree with the NRA and focus for a moment only on their tactics.

The NRA has a constituency that is very passionate and loyal to a single cause: push back against any legislation or politician that supports any restriction on guns. The NRA's position is a minority voice, yet they have managed incredible influence because they can deliver a block of single issue voters and sharp-shoot their attacks. To the NRA constituency, the first requirement of any candidate is to have sympathetic views on gun laws. Any candidate with opposing views is immediately disqualified and subject to attack with all the power that the NRA constituency can throw at them. All other social and economic issues are secondary. This highly effective strategy should be adopted by an independent movement, starting with the single-minded issue of de-corrupting politics. Once that is achieved, an independent movement can move on to other issues.

A platform needs to be highly focused and avoid the distraction traps others have fallen into. For example, the Tea Party started out as a grass roots non-partisan movement around fiscal responsibility; however, the platform was quickly adopted by more hard-right elements and morphed to something very different. For whatever reason, this movement's focus on fiscal responsibility got side-tracked with such issues as gun ownership and illegal immigration that it lost its primary focus.

Despite claims to include Democrats, a Tea Party Democrat is rarer than a white leopard. The Tea Party morphed into what it wanted to morph into, but the issue of fiscal responsibility took on a class warfare position changing the originating premise and diluting focus. The Tea Party has its own influence but quickly lost its bipartisan position in the center. The Tea Party can't possibly inspire cooperation from an extreme conservative position. It can only influence the Republican Party which is not a position of real strength. Further, the Tea Party has only weakened the Right with its brinksmanship "all or nothing tactics" because has insufficient critical mass to effectively pull it off. **If the Tea Party really wanted to achieve its original premise, it should have maintained focus and waited to build critical mass with the right timing to achieve its original goal**.

It is interesting to note that one of the 15 non-negotiable core beliefs of The Tea Party is to eliminate special interest. The Tea Party could be a potential ally in the fight, regardless of how we might feel about their other views. Those who consider other Tea Party views to be unsavory should be careful to not rule out a timely ally if their assistance might determine a decisive battle that captures the primary objective. This is one instance where the high EQ discipline to accept short term pain for long term permanent gain is of critical importance. You must keep in mind that all other governance issues are easier to solve without a CPE if it is truly the will of the people.

D.   It is Show Time

2.   Voters elect the candidate who represents their wants and needs.

Consider voters and candidates filling out a questionnaire based on their position on the issues.   You would expect rational to select a candidate most aligned with their positions; however, the choice of a voter is far more complex.   Voters want to feel a candidate shares their heart, beliefs, struggle, and values.   We want to believe in the person.   We look for qualities that have nothing to do with the issues at all, subjective qualities such as: Are they presidential? Are they honest? Tough? Are they eloquent speakers? We want someone with ambition and a drive to win. We love when they use clever soundbites, especially when used with impeccable timing, and hate anything that sounds prepared and love at least the illusion of spontaneity.   We are seemingly less concerned if a candidate will actually advance our pet issues.   A candidate just wanting them seems to be enough.   We adopt a herd mentality gravitating towards frontrunners and abandoning those with less public support.   We love to be the ones that picked the winning racehorse, so timing and momentum is also valued by the voter.

The election process is a beauty contest where the most electable candidate is handsome, strong, and has an adoring family and lovely spouse that attend church on Sundays.   The candidate is the debate captain from college, with a sense of humor, and can impress us with geopolitical trivia.   It is that person we'd most like to share a cab or beer with and shares our most fundamental values.

I do not want to criticize the criteria in which we voters use to cast their ballots.   It is what it is and will not likely change any time soon. Again, look to the NRA tactics that control a single-issue voting constituency.   They are entirely unemotional when selecting their candidates.   This tactic should be imitated by determining the position of the candidate, the degree of importance when prioritizing tasks, and the candidate's talent to get it done.

About the time of the 2010 mid-term elections, I stepped into a heated debate between two of my employees, when a young white Republican was challenging a black woman over the accomplishments of Barack Obama. She had a hard time articulating why she supported Obama. While I did not take sides, I stepped in to help her form her thoughts. She supported Obama because he gave her hope for a better tomorrow. She voted the black hope ticket. Likewise, when a Catholic friend supported a past right-to-life Republican over the issue of abortion, I had to ask, "What did he actually do to advance your cause?" Did he act or just yap? It did not matter to her, since the Candidate was a Republican and Republicans say they are against abortion.

E.   What is Truth?

John 18:38 (Pontius Pilate)

3.   Candidates must create a perception that they represent wants and needs.

The first criteria necessary to make a rational decision is good information. Unfortunately, we do not demand truth and our decisions are not rational. People are not necessarily interested in the truth; most are interested in personal gain or loss. If a statement does not support their position, they will either ignore it or consider it false. Voters read between the lines, "What's in it for me?" or for those more group minded "What's in it for us?" We all believe that we are above average intelligence and that life would be better if our ideas were heeded (Yep, including me). We think we see a clearer picture of the world than everyone else. When our candidates put themselves in an indefensible position, we are prideful of our choices and will defend and rationalize indefensible positions they take. Liberal pundits are indignant when Republicans misrepresent and conservative pundits are indignant when Democrats misrepresent. These pundits have found a way to justify misrepresentation, but only if it supports their viewpoint - as if the end justifies the means.

Behavioral Economist, Dr. Dan Ariely, found in his clinical studies that **people will lie and feel justified when they believe it is benefiting someone else**. In fact, polygraphs will register lies much less intensely when the respondents feel they are lying for the benefit of others than if lying for their own benefit. Apprehension to lying or guilt wanes the more someone lies. Liars consider themselves to be good people and **will allocate themselves a lying budget** whereas a virtuous person believes he can lie to some extent. If a politician feels that he has done other good deeds in his life, he will allocate himself more of a budget to lie. Politicians will feel more justified lying if they feel others are lying, which perpetuates a lying contagion. The institution of politics demonstrates how ethics can easily drift in a group dynamic. Politics will never be truthful until voters demand it and voice a consequence to lying.

Politicians need only to convince the voter that they are aligned with voter wants and needs; however, convincing does not make it true. Lawyers convince juries all the time. Their job is not to reveal the truth but to zealously protect and pursue within the bounds of the law a client's legitimate interests. It should not be a surprise that so many politicians are lawyers. So long as it is within the law, a politician can and will say or promise anything they like without consequence. The leeway for creating perception is almost boundless. The only way to combat the misperceptions is through fact-checking which is fortunately being used more.

Truth is tricky business. Our brains continuously receive billions of pieces of information look for shortcuts. Our brains often compare information received to stored patterns and quickly make evaluations without fully processing the data. We constantly make assumptions; precisely what magicians exploit during magic tricks. Delve into the world of neuroscience and you will find a cascade of assumed truths that are not factual at all. Optical illusions demonstrate how we are often fooled by our own brain. The best way to arrive at the most sensible truth that most closely aligns with fact is by consensus using some objective method. *James Surowiecki,* in his book *The Wisdom of Crowds*, points out that we can arrive at more accurate solutions when we average multiple data points. But when we are sitting alone in front of our TV set listening to politicians, forming a consensus when we are by ourselves is hard. Who knows if what they are saying is true or not? Like lions trying to separate an impala from the heard, the talking heads on TV pick us off individually for a "share of mind" to convince us of truths that are not facts because we *want* to believe them. Often, we stop scrutinizing and simply look for media that already supports preconceived ideas and we learn nothing.

Rhetoric is a powerful tool, especially amongst the talking heads and politicians and is one reason why the two parties seem so incredibly polarized at the moment and to absolutely hate each other. Again, since the media loves drama that improves rating, they are stoking the fires. Listen to either Sean Hannity or James Carville and you will get the subtext, "We good, they bad." Obama wants everyone reliant on Government; John Boehner wants inner city kids to die of malnutrition. But these are NOT journalists. They are paid entertainers and it might surprise you how many of us do not know the difference.

I used to listen to a Libertarian conservative radio host, Neil Boortz, who took a call from an avid conservative over some wild statement Neil had made the day before. In absolute spite of the caller, Neil explained that he was an entertainer, not a presenter of facts, and that listeners were stupid to believe otherwise. He brazenly went on to say that he gets high ratings for what he says and gets paid handsomely for it, plain and simple. It was one of the most honest responses I have ever heard from a media personality. The caller still did not get it.

It has been said that the first casualty of war is the truth. Currently Republicans and Democrats are at war and have victimized the truth, egged on by the media to boost ratings. Adolf Hitler is quoted as saying, "The great masses of the people will more easily fall victims to a big lie than to a small one." The rhetorical tricks of the trade are more than described here, but these are a few examples.

Once Wrong = Always wrong

Lawyers use this rhetorical tool when cross-examining witnesses. If they can identify an instance where a witness was ever mistaken on facts, they will try to lead the jury to believe that the witness is wrong on all facts. I have heard this argument on talk radio when the computer models miscalculated the impact of a winter storm in NYC. The conclusion was that computer models used to predict weather must be wrong and, therefore, computer models that suggest global warming must be wrong. Regardless of how one feels about global warming, the two have absolutely NOTHING to do with each other. Pick a different argument!

False Inference

If Mitt Romney owns a mutual fund (whose stocks are chosen by professional portfolio managers and not by Mitt Romney) and one of the hundreds of stocks that the mutual fund owns happens to have a factory in China, then Mitt Romney is outsourcing jobs. Regardless of your party affiliations, this is just ridiculous.

Half-truths

Half-truths ignore context. Bills passed in Congress often have "junk" attached to them to gain enough support to pass the bill. To vote "yes" on a bill does not necessarily mean a Congressman or Senator was in support of the junk. It just means that the benefits of the bill were important enough to compromise on the junk for the more important issue. These half-truths come out especially in primaries to paint a tainted view of the opponent. A Republican incumbent may have voted to lower taxes, but an attachment to close a military base might also be in the bill. During the next primary, the opponent will only point out the issue of the military base and make claims that the incumbent is soft on national defense.

Forcing a Binary Answer

In the simplest case, imagine someone asking you, "Have you stopped whipping your children....Yes or No?" You pause for a moment as a binary answer does not fit. The person asks again, "It is a simple question. Just answer the question. It is not more than 9 words, yes or no?"

You can see how a binary answer entraps you if you answer either yes or no. When forced to give binary answers, you are precluded from saying, "I have never in my life whipped my children." You will see this play out in very subtle ways more often than you might imagine as news entertainers start with an agenda and lead their quarry towards a binary trap.

I was disappointed to watch an interview that a news anchor had with Republican candidate, Ben Carson. I was disappointed because I respect the anchor as a journalist but learned that even he was not immune to the urge to mislead the public when he flipped from journalist to entertainer.

The anchor asked the question, "[Mr. Carson], do you think Barack Obama is a REAL BLACK PRESIDENT?" Ben complained about the media trying to play games with candidates, yet the interviewer persisted, "Can't you just answer the question?

How does a black Ben Carson really answer that rhetorical question? What does it even mean? Why is the question even important? Either way Mr. Carson answers is ammo for the media to mischaracterize his answer. In fact, that was the intention of the question. Ben should have answered, He's real, he's black, and he's president. Nice try and shame on you Mr. news man! What the news anchor did was bad, very bad, precisely because the vast majority of the time he is a highly respectable journalist. Switching like that to entertainer is just plain deceptive because he has used his journalistic credentials to subtly slip in bias. It is not like Rush Limbaugh or Jon Stewart who are known to be biased towards their respective ideological viewpoints.

Statistics

Statistics are useful when used properly. Any legitimate statistician worth his salt will note of all assumptions and describe in detail how the test was conducted. Statistics have to be one of the most abused rhetorical tricks in the politician handbook. Politicians flip out sloppy statistics all the time, especially predictive statistics. There is absolutely no accountability and it is plain shameful and nothing short of an outright lie. Fortunately, many truth watchers look for these lies and give truth ratings for claims in the form of "Pinocchios" where the nose grows based on the extent of the lie. What is sad is that liars lie with impunity. It would be nearly impossible to prevent liars from lying since truth is so individually subjective. However, we can certainly do a better job ourselves by studying the accuracy of claims and making them public through consensus (not by some authorized thought police). It is a simple spreadsheet well within our means.

Not only are we lied to, or more politely, mislead; we lie to ourselves. When we talk politics around the water cooler, we too regurgitate unsubstantiated facts because we believe what we want to believe. We have become a country of bull-shiners with our politicians leading the way. Now, even the public has lost the ethic that one's word actually means something.

Objective truths are easy to test using simple scientific method.

However, subjective claims that are more opinion than truth are more difficult to verify and to stop, although they can be identified as opinions. We have way too much technology not to promulgate claims made to the public. We can open source public segregation of public claims into fact, fiction, and opinion with footnotes such as, misuse of statistics or false inference. I would love to see a TV show hosted by a rhetorical expert that reveals tricks used in news and politics without taking sides.

F.   The Business of Media

4.   The perception is communicated through the media.

The news business is like any other business whose primary interest is profit. The more people who watch a particular news program, the higher the ratings, and the higher the ratings, the more advertising dollars that news organization is able to generate. It is that simple. Unfortunately, confusion arises when a media personality is being a journalist, a sensationalist, or an entertainer.

There are of course wonderful journalists.   Journalists that put themselves in harm's way are downright heroic in exposing difficult global issues and have been able to effect real change because of incredible reporting. The media certainly has a role to play. Unfortunately, the public has developed an appetite for sensationalized reality TV and the news industry has followed when they should have taken a stand.   If we see the media as a crusader for public good, we are unfortunately mistaken. The media is a for-profit business and the media is simply delivering what we have asked them to deliver.   When facts differ from the fickle temperament of society, we need the media to re-orient us and it just isn't happening. The media finds it far more profitable to follow the herd and incite the public for profit. News editors are seemingly the same people who edit Reality TV. We have become eager to be insulted and eager to find fault in others, sometimes over the most ridiculous things.

As an example, Marco Rubio was asked, "Which person, other than a politician, would you like to have a beer with?" He answered, "Malala Yousafzai" (the young Nobel Laureate who stood up for women's rights against Sharia Law and was brutally attacked). The press had a field day arguing that she was underage to be drinking and a Muslim. Like wildfire, it was immediately all over the news as the media was simply eager for drama and less concerned with truth. Just think for a moment what was probably in Rubio's head. We all know he honored Malala enough to want to meet and talk with her. Anyone who thought Rubio wanted anything else believes what they want to believe. There is an eagerness to watch someone fail and an eagerness to take offense and now it's blasted all over the news just like Howard Dean's scream heard round the world. The public needs good journalism now more than ever, but the industry is conspicuously lacking ethics.

The trend in media, particularly on the internet, is towards ever increasing outrageousness that attracts attention. Factual news is just plain boring and Yellow Journalism is making a comeback. The public decides what they want to see and hear and, if the public wants to see political candidates fight like a good *Housewives of Wherever*, the media will instigate fights between candidates. If the public wants to see candidates embarrass themselves, the media will ask rhetorical questions to try to trip up candidates. Then, they will rationalize their role as only trying to test the candidate's nimbleness under pressure.

The first two Republican debates of 2016 spent the first 30 minutes simply trying to instigate fights between candidates and barely discussed any issues. The third debate hosted by CNBC was sickening. It is an illusion to think that the media's interest is to reveal truth or to advance the interest of American politics, although the lie is that they would have you think so.

We have an appetite for salacious news and the media delivers. They are our information drug dealers; we are fixed on drama and they deliver the drug. Truth is an afterthought of the media, meted out periodically when the media needs the public to believe that they are credible again and only because credibility influences ratings and profit. It is no wonder politicians play the perception and not the truth when the media does not perform its societal role to educate the public with facts. As opportunists, a politician will latch on to the game of rhetoric that the media instigates, while claiming to be reporting from the sidelines where they can claim plausible deniability. "THEY were fighting, and we were just reporting." But when the challenges to Barack Obama's citizenship gets the same air time as the massacre in Syria, the public gets a disproportionate sense of importance.

The media stirs up our most terrible fears and wicked thoughts for profit. We the public are only victims if we allow it. If we do not want to hear rhetorical garbage from the media, it is up to us to make a change.

The media warps our sense of importance and risk. Ask the general public if they feel safer from violent crime today than they did 20 years ago and most will tell you, no. But, look at the facts.

U.S. Violent Crime Rate^ and Americans' Perceptions of Crime Rate vs. Year Ago

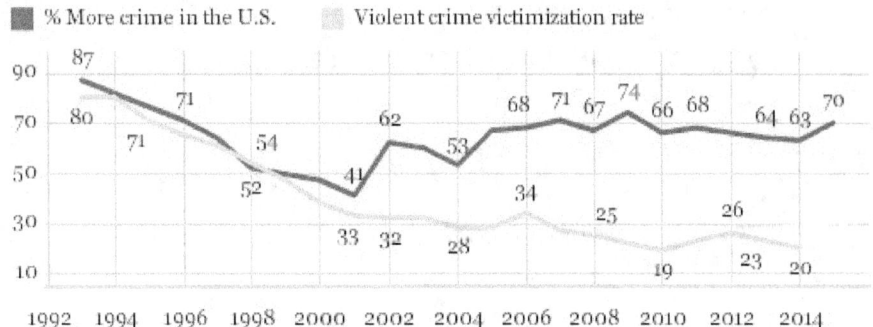

■ % More crime in the U.S.   ■ Violent crime victimization rate

^ Violent crime rate is number of victimizations per 1,000 persons that occurred during the year. Source: Bureau of Justice Statistics, National Crime Victimization Survey, 1993-2014

GALLUP

Misinformation always leads to bad decisions particularly with respect to allocation of resources and public policy. The media as a filter of that information is not reliable. We the public need to know that.

In a free society, the free media is of paramount importance and must be unencumbered. Unfortunately, nothing can be done to force the media to do anything without jeopardizing free press. The only way to check the media is through another media platform. Perhaps a marketing hook is available to lure a new station to fill the current void. I bet the 42% of declared independents might think so. We have Fox on the right, NBC on the left, and CNN trying to be in the middle, but with a snarky lean to the left. However, the issue is not right, left or middle but is good old fashioned ethics in journalism.

If I had a wish list of information media stations it would be these stations that took the concept of no political position as absolute (and it can be done):

- *This Week In Political Rhetoric*
- *No Complaints, Only Solutions*
- *A Psychologists Take on Liberal and Conservative Arguments*
- *Fact Checker*
- *Muckrakers of Political and Societal Corruption*

G. Shaking The Money Tree

5. It takes money to communicate that perception through fundraising.

It is mind blowing how much money is required to run a campaign. Just when we thought we have hit a limit, we double it. Money is essentially spent on advertising with a strategy team, traveling expenses, and advertisements that are so lucrative to the media. A campaign goes nowhere without money. Being the front runner certainly helps to gets free airtime as does being an outrageous personality such as Donald Trump. Early momentum makes it easier to raise funds as donors get no benefit from backing the wrong race horse. Any change to the massive budgets spent on advertising can expect major opposition from the beneficiaries of those dollars, namely the media. As will be discussed later, public funding of elections might be far cheaper in the long run.

H. Quid Pro Quo

6. Fund raising is done by those who want something in return.

Ever wonder who gets invited to the Presidential galas? It is not the guy who donated $50 in an email campaign. Who has the ear of a politician? Who has the active will of a politician? Who gets an appointment to a government position? The joke in Washington is that the Commerce Department is littered with sons and daughters of political contributors as repayment of favors. It is not a free market where we get the best and brightest, rather it is tainted by corruption. What is even more destructive is the resulting corruption in both legislation and government spending.

I had firsthand experience of a quid pro quo event on a social issue. Awhile back an effort was pushed to get Congress to simply recognize that the Turks had killed a million Armenians during World War I. This was one of those terrible events that seemed to get overlooked by history. Hitler was once asked how history would remember his Final Solution and responded, "Did anyone remember the Armenians?" According to the Armenian account, the Turks either outright slaughtered or led families into the desert to starve. Armenians launched a campaign to have Congress simply acknowledge the event that most historians do not contest. Of course, the Turks were opposed an acknowledgment that they would just as soon forget.

My Turkish friend invited me to a dinner with a Congressman. All I really knew about the meeting was that some local Turks were presenting the Congressman with a campaign contribution. First, I was stunned at how little the Congressman said, with so many nonsense phrases, that all seemed scripted and cliché (though he wore a very nice suit). When the meeting was over, my Turkish friend proudly confided that when they first tried to set up the meeting, the Congressman declined saying that he had already had a similar meeting set up with the Armenians. I am not sure quite how the exchange went but it came down to who was donating what amount and the Turks were able to outbid the Armenians. Of course, the parsing of words and body language probably got the deal done, but it was a quid pro quo transaction that flew beneath the radar. Guess how the

Congressman voted on the acknowledgment? Imagine how he would have voted had the Armenians outbid the Turks?

On a local level, I have two friends in real estate who develop raw land. One indicated that he had amazing relationships on the zoning board, whatever that means. The other was not so chummy. He mentioned that when obtaining zoning permits there was a code question, "Is this guy on the team?" meaning, is he a contributor? Donald Trump brazenly boasted that he made dozens of campaign contributions for the benefit of his business. Compared to free market competition through advertising, a targeted campaign contribution can be a very cheap way to generating revenue for any business. It often flies under the radar in the murky world of winks and nods. In many cases, quid pro quo is legally circumvented. The decisions are not free market decisions based on the currency of right or wrong, better or worse. The currency for political decisions is too often, cashola.

I.   Institutionalized Corruption

7. Disproportionate representation challenges the definition of democracy.

As stated earlier, the founding fathers were quite comfortable with the concept of a ruling aristocracy where an elite class could be depended upon to make the right choices for the common citizen. Economic and political favors to the elite were perfectly acceptable practices and a ruling aristocracy's benevolence to the common man were considered a matter of honor and reliable for the norms of the time. It didn't take long for democracy to diverge whereby corruption ran rampant in government. While some protested, corruption was expected and accepted to some extent. Fast forward to today and we live in a far more complex socio-economic environment and corruption, while arguably diminishing, still has had a cumulative negative effect on our democratic process.

The currency for governance is more about money than about the will of the people. The consequences are that we have inflated the role of government and make tainted rather than rational decisions. The undemocratic influence of pay to play politics affects the fairness and efficiency of American governance.

The individual politicians are not necessarily corrupt; rather it is the system that elects them that is corrupt. We have managed to institutionalize corruption by making it either perfectly legal, or so grey that few consequences exist for soft corruption. A politician simply would not be a politician without conforming to institutionalized corruption. Institutionalized corruption is a group entity I have named the CPE with group dynamics that has a personality, a belief system and a Darwinistic will to survive like any other living creature.

Imagine for a moment if there were no paid influence. Public funding of elections, while seemingly expensive and even wasteful to some, is far cheaper in the long run than the current system. Anything that even smells quid pro quo can be eliminated with the stroke of a legislative pen. Our judicial system allows for safeguards such a recusal due to conflict of interest, yet it is conspicuously absent in our legislative process. There are a myriad of good ideas to employ if we only had the will. My strongest hunch is that we are approaching the point where we have the share of the voter minds that appreciate the consequences of corrupt governance. The next step is to lead these minds with the will, motivation, and means to do everything possible to institutionalize integrity or anti-corruption. It is time to plan a strategy.

IV. Strategy Tactics & Timing

The enemy is the Corrupt Political Entity (CPE) which is a group entity with a group dynamic. Understanding the nature of the CPE will be key to defeating it. If we study its routine in the seven steps of the election process, it has vulnerabilities that make it far less invincible than perhaps previously thought. We do not just throw up our hands and yield to the omnipresent beast that looks too big to take down. It all comes down to strategy, tactics, and timing.

The good news is that once the CPE is dismantled, it will be very difficult to resurrect and time is on our side. The CPE is not intentionally unified in its cause; there is no great conspiracy or cooperative effort that is holding it all together. It certainly has no moral authority, which is a core principle of Sun Tzu, and will have a very difficult time defending itself publicly. The CPE is a collection of special interests, devoted to their separate individual causes, be they social or economic. Persistent attacks on a variety of fronts will take it down particularly where it is most vulnerable. Of course, vigilance is required afterwards, but it is a far easier battle to fight.

To expect some epic single battle that would defeat the CPE once and for all would be unreasonable. The battle would be one of attrition. Occasionally, fights will occur on an open battlefield. An independent movement can actively attack the CPE but the CPE can only resist an attack. The CPE is not capable of launching a unified attack on its own, although its ability to resist is quite formidable. **Its strategy is to survive and its tactics are to deceive, confuse, and outlast the opposition until they lose the will to fight**.

As in any fight, timing is critical. Soldiers need victories to maintain a motivated army and the tempo of a fight draws the attention of others. We pick the battlefields. We corner the CPE into an indefensible position by isolating the issue of corruption. We pick the timing especially since we have the advantage with the ability to attack while the CPE only has the power to resist. Since much of our corruption is perfectly legal, the first step is to make it illegal.

A. Know Thy Cause and Build an Army

In Washington, there is an asphalt lobby and a concrete lobby. Both are motivated to see more highway bills get passed as it means more business for both lobbies. These two lobbies are not concerned whether the country needs more roads, more government spending on roads is better for both lobbies. These lobbies would certainly oppose legislation for lighter cars since this would mean less repaving or re-cementing of roads and less business for the two lobbies. These two lobbies take the position that more roads and more maintenance of roads are good. The two lobbies will also lobby as competitors such that their slice of the pie is as big as possible. As far as the lobbyists are concerned it is up to the politician to make the right decision because lobbyists are not in the ethics business. However, when money is involved, decisions become tainted.

An independent movement takes no position on the optimal number of new road projects or takes a position on whether lighter cars are a good idea or not. It simply takes the position that paid influence leads to bad economic and social decisions. If the idea were sound, paid influence would not be needed at all.

In another example, consider the NRA fight to preserve its interpretation of second amendment rights. The Independent movement does not take a position on gun laws. **The agenda of the Independent movement simply takes paid influence out of the equation.** If the voting public decides that semi-automatic weapons and large capacity clips are a good idea, so be it, but it will be the will of the people and not the paid will of a few.

Opposing views will still debate the issues, and quite frankly should. The only goal is to remove corruption from the decision-making process and let the chips lie where they may. This gives an independent movement a huge advantage over the corruptors. First, corruptors do not stand on moral ground which is hard to defend. Second, it opens up a two-front war in which corruptors will have a very difficult time defending. Fighting both issue adversaries and anti-corruption efforts at the same time is a difficult two-front war. Those fighting issues influenced by corruption should appreciate an independent movement, similar to a rigged fight where a referee steps in and eliminates the cheating. The cheater will resist, but the referee will have the support of the disadvantaged fighter even with a referee who does not care who wins. Gather up everybody losing because of corruption and convince them that, while the Independent movement is not taking sides on their cause, they are natural allies.

With 42% of the voting public unaligned with either political party, they will remain apathetic until there is momentum through leadership and proven victories. **The easiest recruits are those fighting issues where corrupt forces are disadvantaging them.** Like the disadvantaged fighter, they may be convinced that their only chance of a fair fight is to align with an independent movement that will take the first step in peeling back the first layer of obstruction. Paid influence is detrimental to their cause. Help us remove paid influence and good luck on your issue.

Again, it is critical not to get bogged down in the issues despite the temptation to do so. They will resolve themselves in their own way, fairly and rationally.

B.   Divide Defect & Unite

The goal is to bring conservatives and liberals together for more cooperative governance. To perpetually divide ourselves does not further anyone's interest. Politicians have been sucked into the larger group dynamic of the CPE. We are not after the politicians or the parties; the CPE is the target. The distinction is a critical point to remember and we better know the difference. If our sites are taken off the CPE as the real enemy, then the battle will be lost on the strategy table. We need politicians if we are to have a representative democracy, to change the laws that have institutionalized corruption, and to work cooperatively and find common ground wherever possible to achieve results. We are only trying to eliminate the toxic corruption of the CPE.

Consider a strategy to separate the polarizing *hardliners* from *centrists* with a good old fashioned branding campaign. By identifying who is who, the Independent movement could appeal to the centrists to separate from the hardliners and cooperate with the centrists from the other party, perhaps forming a *Cooperative Centrist Caucus*. The Cooperative Caucus might have stronger utility to a politician than the individual parties as quite often hardliners are a liability to centrists. Labeling politicians is only mirroring the views of the voters. Make no mistake; this is a slow drip branding strategy that takes time to take effect. It has already started to leak in to the public vernacular, but now it is time to step on the gas.

While Independents are nowhere near critical mass to elect an Independent President, think of what Independents could achieve with just 6 Senators and 25 House Members? They would be precisely in the right position to have tremendous influence as the marginal vote. A center coalition has far more power than extreme coalitions. Find those districts where electing independents is a real possibility and victory could be very possible with relatively few resources. Unlike Independents, Republicans and Democrats need a majority to control Congress. **Independents need only to control the marginal vote, analogous to being the "center of gravity" of Congress.** That is amazing leverage! A tightrope walker can do anything with his arms and legs so long as he keeps that plum-sized center of gravity over the wire. You could broadcast this strategy to both Republicans and Democrats and there is still nothing they could do to stop it.

In game Theory, economists study rational behavior under quirky scenarios.

Imagine three gunfighters in a three-way fight to the death. In round one, each picks a target and shoots. Whoever is still alive, picks another target and this continues until one man (or no man) is standing. Gunfighter A has a 90% accuracy, B = 70%, and C = 40%. Who has the best chance of survival? As it turns out statistically, C has the best chance since the others are likely to die in the first round.

Remember that a prime objective is for Independents to end polarizing ideology and encourage more cooperation. As the marginal voters controlling the center of gravity, Independents would have a stronger voice if the other parties decide to keep fighting. Independents might even encourage the other gunfighters to holster their guns and head for the saloon to work it out.

C. Gathering Assets

Strategy is key to winning a battle. Sun Tzu argues that **battles are won and lost on the strategy table prior to any battle.** The only reason for a fight is because one combatant does not recognize that he has already lost. Imposing your will using the threat of overwhelming force without a battle is the best possible outcome since no resources are wasted.

Imagine if 10 wealthy Americans amassed a treasure chest to end corruption in politics and seeded Congress with anti-corruption crusaders for a better America. You may ask if this is hypocritical since we are talking about paid influence? You betcha it is! *The Cave dwellers ultimately had to use the threat of force to end Gyork's forceful stealing of their women.* This is death to corruption and it will be a knife fight. Let's paint a crazy hypothetical scenario.

With a formidable treasure chest, the sitting politician is faced with the scenario, capitulate to the corruption reform laws or lose the next election. **Any rational politician would capitulate without a penny ever spent.** Remember the first goal of any politician is to get elected. The threat needs to be real and credible with perhaps an isolated demonstration to convince the doubtful might be in order.

I do not expect 10 wealthy Americans are itching to open their wallets at the moment. However, if a grass roots independent movement reached critical mass, the benevolent wealthy class (and I suspect there are many) might recognize the enormity such a contribution to America and perhaps to the rest of the world. Just the threat of power should be enough to tip the balance, if used at a critical moment. The key is to attract a heroic wealthy as the only possible counterweight to paid influence and to do it wisely and inexpensively. Many wealthy Americans are massive benefactors anyways and their causes are also obstructed by corruption. For example, Bill & Melissa Gates and Mark Zuckerberg have taken up the cause to advance education. They both face friction from corruptors standing in the way of sensible ideas. A better strategy might be to fight corrupt obstruction to sensible education.

Consider the following steps:

1. Establish a clear a narrowly defined single issue objective.

2. Organize leadership chapters at the state level

3. Build a core dedicated army by consolidating existing groups.

    • Anti-corruption groups.

    • Fact checking websites

    • Leaders in social media

4. Attract grass roots donor money to the cause

5. Inform the public with a marketing campaign to attract new members

    • Any interest group disadvantaged by pay-to-play politics

    • Attract any like-minded public personality with influence

6. Attract big donor money to create a credible determined threat

7. Launch a broader campaign to attract declared Independents

8. Wait, wait, wait, until the timing is right

    • Look for a spark that can ignite a fire keg

    • When certain you can achieve results

    • When able to, create fast contagious momentum

    • If necessary, demonstrate your power to influence votes

9. Convince or fight

As a note, we should expect the natural tendency to corrupt will permeate even anti-corruption groups. In step 3 above, I recommend consolidating existing anti-corruption groups. Consolidating groups often require consolidating leadership. Will the interest of the leadership be to advance the cause of anti-corruption or might that interest conflict with the leadership's desire to be leaders? The authenticity of an Independent movement will be critical for its success.

D.   Attack Where Your Opponent is Weakest

A fantastic strategy is to take advantage of the lower voter turnout during the midterm elections because a single-issue voting block would have greater impact. During general election, voter turnout has been about 56%, but during midterm elections, voter turnout drops to 38%. That is less competition for votes and more impact that an independent movement could have. The same number of Congressional seats is up for re-election every two years (33% of the Senators and 100% of the House members). That is a huge bang for the buck to focus effort on the mid-terms. Remember, once election reform is enacted, it is VERY difficult to undo. Think about how long it took to disqualify Congress from insider trading. Progress is made quickly in the mid-term election, but it only becomes lasting when you can influence the more popular election that has more participation.

E.   A Clear Agenda

Can I Get A Witness?

The very best place to start is to examine the tools of corruption and come up with laws that corruptors would least like to see enacted?

Corruptors hate transparency and do not want witnesses. It is no accident that violent crime is more likely to occur in a remote parking lot late at night rather than on aisle seven of the neighborhood grocery store in the afternoon. It is one reason why crime has dropped in the United States. Surveillance cameras are everywhere and most folks can video directly off their mobile phones.

Transparency flirts with the rights of privacy, but in this case social benefits far outweigh the restriction of liberty. Liberty is where corruptors operate best. Imagine if a politician had to keep a publicized log of every meeting or phone call he took from a donor giving more than the individual limit of $2,700. Yeah, and remove the loopholes that allow special interest use of 3rd parties to bundle donors or transfer monies between politicians. "Soft" money should be considered a campaign contribution in every sense such as paid speech, private loans that are made at below market rates with default forgiveness, contribution to a presidential library, or use of a private jet. Until more robust laws are enacted, soft money should be fully disclosed. There is nothing wrong with meeting with a Senator, just write it down in the log and publish it for everyone to see. I suppose foreign governments might just have a few sensitive things to discuss, but they should not be making direct or indirect contributions.

Short of making corruption illegal, transparency laws are the most effective tool for making it much more difficult. When an independent movement gets stuck on getting proper legislation, transparency laws are the next best thing. Of course, there will be obstructionists to transparency laws, arguing that everybody has secrets and that secrecy is important to protect privacy. It is a ruse to protect corruptors.

Recusal

Recusal is an outstanding model used by the judicial system. When a judge has some personal interest in a case he must recuse himself due to potential bias. When someone effectively contributes above some designated amount, politicians should be obliged to recuse themselves from issues concerning that donor. If it is too restrictive to the politician, then do not accept the donation.

Strict Ethics

Remember the move *The Untouchables* starring Kevin Costner as Eliot Ness? Chicago was rife with corruption at all levels when Al Capone ran the town with impunity. The Untouchables was an elite group of FBI agents that had been screened for their incorruptibility. We desperately need to strengthen Congressional ethics.

Sometimes It Is Cheaper To Pay

Currently, political campaigns are a side show circus act. Unfortunately, politicians have just too much money to be used bombarding us with so much nonsense. Some countries rein in the deluge of campaigning by defining shorter campaign windows.

Public funding of campaigns is pricey in the short run but far cheaper in the long run. We already have government TV such as CSPAN. Why not find a way to grant air time to federal, state, and local candidates based on polling data. Should a candidate harness some threshold popularity, give them a worthy fixed budget to run their campaigns. Similarly, provide a public website for candidates to get out the message. Let it be generous and we still save a mountain of loot on irrational decisions by our rule makers. With such public funding, we can eliminate pay to play politics altogether with campaign finance reform.

A Clean Retirement

Until we can create the consensus necessary to amend the constitution, politicians should view politics as public service and not as a platform to later pull the jackpot lever. Upon retirement, any and all campaign moneys still in the coffers must be returned to the US Treasury immediately without exception. A politician would be prevented from directing moneys to any organization whatsoever. This would eliminate the old *let's form a think tank and I will pay myself a salary or expenses until the money runs dry* scenario. Retired politicians should be prohibited from any contact with any sitting politician for which the retired politician is compensated with either real dollars or soft dollars. Upon retirement, they are free to make paid speeches to private organizations and receive book royalties, but that is it.

End Rules of Obstruction

The Hastert Rule, also known as the "majority of the majority" rule, is an informal governing principle used by Republican Speakers of the House of Representatives since the mid-1990s. **The Hastert Rule says that a Republican Speaker will not schedule a floor vote on any bill that does not have majority support within his or her party - even if the House would likely vote to pass it**. The rule prevents the minority party from passing bills with the assistance of a small number of majority party members.

The Hastert Rule was used when Obama asked for war authorization against ISIS. The vote never went to the floor, even though it was likely to pass. Republicans would not be held accountable for either voting for or against a bill because voting was blocked altogether by the Hastert Rule. Republicans blocked the bill because they wanted to undermine Obama without the accountability of voting against the Bill.

Any law, rule, or tradition of Congress that prevents a vote, is undemocratic. In fact, a law should be enacted whereby House and Senate leaders are obliged to bring a bill to a vote with just 40% support. It is important for getting issues on the table and see where everyone stands rather than allowing politicians to hide for political gain and a powerful way to emphasize loyalty to democratic process over political party.

Bundling bills with unrelated issues should either not be allowed or Congress should be able to vote on unrelated components of a bill. It is a radical departure from a system that politicians are so convinced is necessary. In 1996, the president had a line item veto that was ruled unconstitutional in 1998, so something like this requires a constitutional amendment to give both the president and those voting in Congress the ability to vote on components of a bill instead of a bundle.

Amend the Constitution If Necessary

Based on the Citizens United ruling by the Supreme Court, it is time to amend the constitution to enact campaign finance reform if it conflicts with the First Amendment. Paid influence should not infringe upon the fundamental democratic principle of one person, one vote. If the First Amendment written in the 18th Century is inadequate today, then re-write it.

F.   Donald Trump

The most interesting result of the 2016 election has been that of Donald Trump and his appeal to voters.   Die hard Republicans automatically voted for Trump because he rose from their tribe.   What is most fascinating was that his appeal to so many frustrated marginal voters made him President.   I believe these independents have been frustrated for a very long time with the general state of American politics and see a candidate who appears immune to the rules of the game.   He rattles a system that voters have felt to be impossible to change and this gave them hope for other possibilities.   What could be better than a businessman who is not a politician?   Despite his outrageousness and alternative facts, voters were frustrated enough to gamble and gamble BIG.   Trump punctuated the ideal that what was impossible in the past might just possible with a Teflon candidate who can double talk his way through the media gauntlet.   Trump may not be the right kind of different, but he is certainly different and some voters were so eager for different they voted for Trump who seemed to survive scrutiny with his uncanny ability to brand simple messages.

The biggest take away point is not about Trump, rather it is about the powerful discontent of Independents motivating their desire to be led somewhere different.   It indicates that Independents are more than ripe for a well-led Independent movement.

Like him or not, Trump entered the Presidency under unprecedented conditions.   All conventional rules were broken.   He is not really a Republican or a Democrat and politicians are off balance.   Upon his inauguration, Trump was in the catbird seat.   It does not matter who Trump really is.   This is where Sun Tzu would say, *Build Trump a golden bridge and lead him to it.*

Trump wants to be great and adored for it.   All presidents do.   He has already campaigned on "draining the swamp".   We just need to help him understand what that means to us so we can genuflect to his greatness.

Hopefully, Trump will soon learn that unlike business, politics requires consensus.   For the time being, Trump has surrounded himself with advisors salivating to enact legislation for which there is thin support. They are thinking that because Republicans are in a power position that this is their chance to realize their vision. Perhaps they can temporarily, but the next time there is a power shift to the Democrats, their efforts are likely to be undone. Obamacare is a great example. Obama jammed through healthcare legislation with disregard to Republican concerns when Democrats were in a power position. Now that Republicans are in control, they are working to undo it. If Trump convinced the public first by building consensus, he would have less public outcry and legislation would stick. It is a question of EQ and patience that seems to be lacking with this ADD president. It was seductive to think that a businessman could come in and shake things up with the authority enjoyed by a CEO, but that is not how politics work, especially international politics.

I could spend hours on the Trump phenomenon. Let's just say that while the goal is to dismantle corruption and polarization, we have to work with what we have. He may learn on the job and surprise half of us, or he may fail miserably and surprise the other half. Time will tell. What is more productive than complaining about Trump or defending Trump is to lead him where we want him to go with a flashy lure that appeals to Trump. If by some chance Trump can be convinced it is in his personal interest to end corruption and polarization, he will be the first to board the train.

How do you convince Trump? That is not an easy task since he is not inclined to listen to views he doesn't already agree with. Remember that fear is the greatest motivator for persuasion? We employ the five steps described earlier, hope he is paying attention, and pray for a miracle.

1. Mr. Trump, you have a problem. Your approval rating is in the toilet and everyone is nipping at your heels. Your credibility is becoming more and more suspect and you are losing those that previously supported you.

2. It is a serious problem. Without good will, you won't be able to get anything done at home. Protesters are mobilizing. Republicans are under pressure. If there is an international crisis, who will you call for support? Your legacy could one day read absolute failure and your business brand is in serious jeopardy.

3. There is urgency to fix this problem. What happens if Republicans turn on you, or international allies? The midterm elections are fast approaching. A Democratic Congress is not only unfriendly to you, they could be dangerous. Remember that other presidents have faced impeachment for issues of credibility when they were low on political currency. At best, do you want to lose Congress in 2018 or be voted out in 2020? What does that do to the Trump brand?

4. Dispel naysayers. Are your advisors serving your interest? Do they have you throwing Hail Mary's? Do they face the same consequences you do? Are they building consensus or destroying good will by jamming THEIR agendas? Perhaps they were good election advisors but bad political advisors. Let's rethink these people who are using you for personal gain.

5. Enter as the Rainmaker. Hopefully, it is early enough to fix this. Let's rebuild your goodwill and credibility. Throw away that twitter thing for a month or two. We'll slow down and allow those great ideas of yours to percolate before speaking. Let's fight battles we can win for which there is consensus. Everyone hates bickering and corruption. Let's go back to that great idea you had about draining the swamp that seemed to pull people together. We can float a trial balloon and gauge public reaction to a de-corruption agenda. They will be so wowed by you pulling off the impossible; they will offer you babies to kiss. You have a better chance of getting it done than anyone before you. You will be safe with a mountain of political currency. Your image will improve, will have more cooperation, and your brand will rocket to new heights.

V. Beyond The Political Objective

If we were to remove corrupt influences and cooperate more, we could make decisions more rationally, be far more efficient, and struggle less. We would have a more secure economy, a happier outlook that tomorrow will be better than today and get along better. Our environment will be cleaner, healthier and more sustainable. We would earn more respect as a world leader and feel safer both at home and abroad. We would have a more equitable society that places no boundaries on earned reward, yet is far more compassionate than it is today. We might understand each other better, trust each other more, and feel more comfortable with Libertarian ideals. We would be more morally pure, dignify each other with a fair playing field, and be less polarized. We could push the reset button and have a fresh start taking a giant leap in social evolution.

Notice the words used above. They both describe Conservative and Liberal Values. I'm convinced that we can cooperate and can end our battle of binary ideology. We all want to feel safe, achieve goals, and be happy.

CONSERVATIVES – uses words like: character, virtue, discipline, tough it out, get tough, tough love, strong, self-reliance, individual responsibility, backbone, standards, authority, heritage, competition, earn, hard work, enterprise, property rights, reward, freedom, intrusion, interference, meddling, punishment, human nature, traditional, common sense, dependency, self-indulgent, elite, quotas, breakdown, corrupt, decay, rot, degenerate, deviant, lifestyle.

LIBERALS – use words like: social forces, social responsibility, free expression, human rights, equal rights, concern, care, help, health, safety, nutrition, basic human dignity, oppression, diversity, deprivation, alienation, big corporations, corporate welfare, ecology, ecosystem, biodiversity, and pollution.

If you are fixed on ideology, only about 50% of the remainder of this book will make sense to you; the rest will just make you mad. I invite you to liberate yourself from ideology for a moment as we apply these seven principles to current social, economic and world issues:

1. Remove corrupt influences and while preserving as much liberty as absolutely possible.

2. Consider both liberal and conservative points of view.

3. Apply democratic principles and self-determination.

4. Apply free-market principles adjusted for economic externalities.

5. Solutions must be efficient, sustainable and in our long-term interest.

6. Promote voluntary organic compassion that is more lasting than forced compassion. We are obliged not to corrupt, but not obliged to involuntarily help others we have not corrupted.

7. Maximize the benefit to the group while not forcing equalization.

8. Consider the effects on the overall ecosystem.

I don't presume to have a monopoly on truth or that the following solutions could not be improved upon. My hope is that by looking at these issues from an oblique perspective, we might think outside the box and prompt a dialogue. Perhaps you would like to contribute your own ideas If we want real change, we have to think differently if we expect a different result. Finally, before we can efficiently solve these issues, we should have first addressed political corruption.

A. Make Problems Smaller

The Republican Party has long held the position that we should reduce the size of the federal government and pass more control to the states making the problems smaller and solutions more local. Californians and Texans are entirely different animals and all-encompassing federal programs do not necessarily fit both preferences. Having separate programs for each would have a better fit. Smaller problems are easier to solve.

The best argument for moving power to the 50 states is that we have the opportunity to conduct 50 different experiments. If New Hampshire adopts a health care program that is far superior to Kansas, then Kansas can decide to change its health care model to that of New Hampshire model…or not.

The only role of the federal government would be to regulate the interstate component where the actions of one state might affect that of another. For example, should Oregon legislate a model state program where it enjoys a surplus budget and life is too good to be true, it would be unfortunate to have those in a failed state migrate to Oregon without some accounting of associated costs. Such a migration dilutes the positive benefits earned by Oregonians and concentrates the problems of those left behind in problem states. Since this is a more Conservative concept, let's emphasize how it might fit Liberal ideals by being more local, grass root efforts will have more voice, the data will teach us to be more efficient, and Liberals will have a better opportunity to see their prescribed solutions realized.

B. What to do With Thieves?

Corruptors are thieves and the cost to society is enormous. Think of all the costs associated with theft, theft prevention, and theft enforcement. We need a convincing deterrent to deliberate theft. Personally, I am in favor of thieves not necessarily going to jail but paying back some multiple of the theft.

Willful deception that leads to a victim's loss is theft. Why Bernie Maddoff's estate has any assets at all is bewildering. The Enron executives, who cooked the books for personal gain and lost huge sums of investor money, went to jail, yet still have personal assets. O.J. Simpson has barely paid a dollar of the $33MM settlement against the Goldman family, yet regularly enjoys a round of country club golf.

I like the idea that consequences should fall into categories for deliberate theft. At a minimum, deliberate theft should require a 300% payback to be divided equally between the victim, the enforcement agency, and lawyer + court costs (you must be careful not to incent false accusers although they, too, would be subject to theft laws). For the real egregious cases, let there be some very high percentage payback such as a public official siphoning funds into his personal account. No wealth of the thief would be off limits including foreign wealth, a Florida home, car, pension or IRA.

Thieves would re-evaluate the upside of stealing if the consequences were unacceptable. They think twice with more transparency and well-funded enforcement.

Fraud

Corruption is a form of theft. Recall a previous statement that all sin, be it lying, cheating, or even an assault can be considered as some form of corruption. Corruptors hate transparency and will deceive outright or lie by omission of important facts. A thief likes a vulnerable target and certainly wants to use clandestine tactics to avoid discovery and, of course, consequence. We throw around terms such as caveat emptor, "let the buyer beware", as if to say that we live in a Darwinistic world where the strong will and should devour the weak. It is of course harmonious with our nature as animals, but humans are different in that we can intellectualize beyond our primal instincts.

On Wall Street, the attitude is *en garde*; if you are stupid enough to believe me, then tough beans. The truth I lead you to believe is up to you to verify in a cryptic prospectus. It seems to be the only practical way to run a financial industry, after all, how can any salesman really know if a client really understands or not? This is where regulation steps in. But consider two types of law. There is both specific law and conceptual.

In the case of Orange County, the regulators used specific law with rules that were believed to prevent the high-risk trades. Wall Street loves specific law since they are clever at spotting loopholes. A conceptual regulation would have been far more appropriate. Conceptual law covers unforeseen changes while specific law only covers what is known at the time. Ultimately, society pays the cost of fraud. We would be better served going after fraudsters than going after the productive rich for the sake of being rich.

Predators

Title loans are another example of corruption. Usury laws vary from state to state that prohibit charging obscene interest rates, often referred to as predatory lending. In Georgia, the usury rate is 16% APR. However, title loans are written in such a way that they are not technically loans, although for all intents and purposes, they are. Borrowers pay about 25% per month or 300% per annum. Most title companies know desperate borrowers are unlikely to repay the cost to get their cars back. In fact, title companies make more money if they are not repaid. Let's say a car is worth $3,000 in a quick sale transaction. The title company will loan less than 50% of the value of the quick sale price, let's say $1,000. After just one month the borrower owes $1,250 and if he or she is unable to pay, the car is repossessed and quick sold for $3,000. Even though the borrower only owed $1,250 (a crime to begin with), the title company can legally keep the entire $3,000 from the repossession. Do the math on that rate of return.

My neighbors in our business complex are the collection arm of Title Loans. The windows are blackened and there are no identifying signs anywhere. They do not want transparency. They deliberately maintain an invisible stealth profile.

We can say tough tacos to the desperate borrower and explain that he or she should have understood the contract better or was just stupid to have taken the money, *caveat emptor*. But we are all affected by what just happened. That desperate person is now more desperate and we know that desperate people can be dangerous inviting crime. At the very least, society will need to step in with some social welfare to feed that desperate person while the predator flies his private jet to the Bahamas for the weekend. Forget right or wrong for just a moment. Are you happy to see your taxes subsidize a predator and his victim?

C. Social Corruption

Race - Patterns and Empowerment

Race issues can be improved by teaching the skills necessary for economic participation. Participation gives people value worth protecting so they become vested. By being vested they will participate more effectively in solutions. Economic power yields influence so that minority groups can better set the rules.

Overt racism is for a different audience whom I do not want to know, but it is not the most damaging aspect of racism today. **What is far more damaging than conspicuous racism is the quiet racism of indifference and avoidance.**

For many of us (black or white), we stay in our neighborhoods and they stay in theirs. We hire our own and they hire their own. We simply segregate ourselves physically, socially, economically, and emotionally. Racism occurs on two levels and certainly happens in two directions. Whites have just as many preconceived notions of blacks as blacks have towards whites. Racial profiling is a double-edged sword. At another level, both groups reinforce segregationist attitudes within their respective groups. Blacks do not seem to want to appear too white and whites do not want to appear too black, lest they get raised eyebrows within their own groups. The practical question is twofold. First, is there corruption based on race, which should be addressed if we are truly driven by principle? Second, would society be better off if we were to close the economic gap between whites and those of color?

I suspect that the independent voice would like to see those of color improve their lot in life though there is frustration with the game plan. Unfortunately, many in the black leadership have exploited the situation for their own personal gain. The Jesse Jackson's and Al Sharpton's of the world have squarely led their people down a cul-de-sac, enriching themselves in the process. They pander to the crowds who cheer them on as they are being led nowhere. Trouble in the world of race is big money for these scoundrels and they are charismatic corruptors. Leaders like John

Lewis, whether one agrees or disagrees with policies, are far more authentic. John Lewis is a man to be respected and honored because he is genuine. Colin Powell is also a wise leader, but for whatever reason, has opted out of the political dialogue. Few men are as honorable and authentic as these great patriots.

Of course, race is a sensitive topic, but I want to hit it head-on by looking at where we are, where we want to be, and how to get there. First, this discussion is only for those who would like to see people of color improve their lot in life. Folks that hate are encouraged to leave the room.

For those of you still left, I am going to be so presumptuous as to generalize independent-minded white attitudes towards people of color. Race is not an issue of skin color but is an issue of culture. The hard facts are that a child born to a black family is more likely to grow up in a lower socio-economic stratum of society, are more likely to be raised in a single-family home where the family glue comes from the women with absentee fathers, are more likely to be exposed to family and neighborhood violence, and are less likely to be supervised. Consequently, they are less likely to perform as well in school, have higher dropout rates and are not as well prepared for the economic world that would provide them personal power as adults. It should be no surprise that anyone with this sort of upbringing would be disadvantaged. They are told that whites are responsible and that there is some conspiracy designed to keep people of color in this recurring loop of despair.

I'm afraid there is no great conspiracy that I know of by the white machine within the independent constituency. **Whites simply don't understand what it is really like to be black in America and avoid what they don't understand.** Overt racism is isolated to white trash. Quiet racism, though, is ubiquitous amongst all of us and is manifested in apathy, indifference, and voluntary segregation based on misunderstanding and fear. Most recognize social value to all by elevating lower economic groups within society. After all, ANYONE with little to lose will become desperate.

We exhibit the most damaging aspects of racism with avoidance and indifference. Human beings have evolved a system of profiling that is of evolutionary benefit to the survival of the species. **Profiling is perfectly rational and we ALL do it ALL the time**. You meet someone on the street and your first evaluation is safe or dangerous. Once that is resolved, we move up to higher social qualities as they become relevant such as, would I want to invite this person to my home or hire them in my business. But often, we have absolutely no idea who this person is and are forced to act on incomplete information. If we had the time, we could sit down and hash out who they really are, but we do not have that time luxury. We make split second determinations to fill in the information gaps by comparing patterns with our brain's library of patterns, based upon experience, either real or imagined. We naturally avoid risk and generally navigate what we feel to be the safest possible path.

If I walk past a woman in a mall tickling her baby in a stroller, she fits a pattern. I do not expect to be harmed or that she will ask me for a donation to some cause. She fits a pattern and in a split-second I can make an evaluation. Sometimes I might be surprised, but, more often than not, I'll get it right. If I am in a parking lot outside a convenience store at night and I see four rowdy young rednecks wearing sunglasses drinking Jack Daniels wrapped in a paper bag, I would have quite a different reaction. We all would. The more that the person fits our impression of safe, the more we would choose to interact. The more the person fits social patterns familiar to us, the deeper we will interact.

In Redondo Beach, I saw a policeman walk up to a car with a mother and child with his hand hovering over his holster, approaching the car as if there was danger. I thought about what the officer might have experienced in the past that made him so cautious. Could it have been just training or perhaps he had an experience with someone he thought to be harmless but who pulled a gun on him? I will never know. Every time we get pulled over by a policeman, we are subject to all the experiences he has had pulling over other drivers. It is not fair, but it is perfectly rational. Filling in impartial information with patterns is a Darwinistic quality that kept us safe and helped us to survive as a species. The more positive information we can project to a stranger, the more likely they are to view us positively. I sure would not wear a bandana and a biker vest that says, "Anarchy or Death" and expect to be treated the same as if I wore a suit and tie. **The point is that, if we don't want to be judged based upon a pattern, don't**

fit the pattern. In addition, for all those out there creating negative patterns, you are harming all those behind you who happen to match the pattern.

We are programmed to pattern profile. It is NOT fair, but it is a fact and any primal behavior is too deeply engrained to try to change. Some think we can mandate the end to pattern profiling, but we are naive to think that our primal tendency to pattern profile will ever change. We can only pretend it is not there, but it is like asking someone to stop hiccupping. It must be considered a given and any solution will work around this given axiom.

I am fascinated by the topic of race and speak openly to people of color with whom I have become friends. In my business, we had a vendor of color who happened to be just terrible. He could not solve any problems and mostly just dropped by to shake hands and talk about things we were just too busy to listen to. Nonetheless, we have held this business relationship for over 10 years and shared a good bit. As a businessman, he was fluff and little stuff but a likable guy.

He explained to me how his company was racist and that he kept a dossier on everyone in management, as he fully expected to engage them one day in some race-biased case. When the time was ripe, he would contact Jesse Jackson, make a lot of money on a pre-trial settlement, and move on. In addition, he would be heralded by the black community as a champion for the cause.

I had this discussion with him, "Johnny, you had better be right before you do something like this. Let's say that Jesse flies down to stand by your side and you win some settlement. You do realize that everyone of color who comes behind you to these company managers looking for a job will be adversely affected by what you've done? You had better be right about this and it does not mean that you should not defend yourself if you are. You should certainly think this through and have a heck of a case or you are screwing the pooch for your black brethren. You will have created a pattern in someone's mind that they will use to compare others that look like you, walk like you, and talk like you."

Anyone of ANY color who wants power needs economic participation. If the keys of economic participation are held by others, then they set the rules. When I worked on Wall Street, I had to project something different than the parochial beach volleyball player I was because of the scrutiny of every perception. After all, I would be interacting with portfolio managers and executives, who were very smart people with a certain business culture and a lot of money. I had to dress a certain way, talk a certain way, with a predictability that would give my managers confidence that I could do the job and was not some wildcard. If I did not like it, I could work elsewhere.

I could have complained to human resources that Lehman Brothers should be more tolerant of who and what I really was. And let's assume I got it done and human resources made a tolerance rule for beach idiots like me. It would not change a thing though perhaps they would not be allowed to fire me. They would shuffle me off to the side with resentment where I could do no harm. Human resources, despite their best intentions to diversify, would have done me a disservice. I would have won my battle but lost the war and hurt the opportunities of anyone who remotely smelled like the Pacific Ocean.

Profit is a powerful motivator to those who hold the keys of economic participation. If I could make Lehman Brothers buckets of money, they would not care what I was. Once I earned a name for myself and proved indispensable, I could start making the rules, wear a hula dress, and talk like a hillbilly, but until then, like everyone else, I need to fit a pattern of expectation.

While not fair, the white corporate culture dominates economic participation. It is a harsh fact, for now. People of color are not to abandon their own culture; in fact, they should thoroughly embrace it. It would greatly help to be bilingual and bicultural in both cultures and to nimbly adapt to their environments just like I had to at Lehman Brothers. Adaptation is pragmatic. Adaptation is not selling out as many black leaders espouse. Adaptation is not to be confused with taking on a second-class role in ANY way. Adaptation is not kissing ass. Adaptation fulfills expectations in a calculated manner with particular goals in mind. We all want opportunities from those holding the economic keys to the kingdom.

Once the doors have been opened and achievement is earned, new rules can be made.

Seeking economic participation is the goal and being bilingual and bicultural is only part of the equation. **Earning the right skill set with both knowledge and discipline is the second ingredient to meaningful change.** The question is how to reach that goal from the disadvantaged starting point described earlier. Now that's a tough one. First, not a penny should be spent on trying to equalize and impose changing of our rational tendency to profile that took mankind a million years to develop. It is far wiser to cooperate with human nature than it is to fight it.

The solution is to create earned economic empowerment with real value. If equalization is mandated, it will fail or only produce a temporary illusion of success. The most effective starting point is with the youth who are most malleable to change. We can experiment with ideas that will keep disadvantaged kids busy for most of the day around role models who will make a difference.

My good son has ADD and, when he got into high school, got into some minor trouble at school and rebelled in a way that a 16yr old can. He was at the point of giving up and decided not to try anymore. His behavior quickly began to spiral out of control. We enrolled him in military school where he flourished. Cadets earned privilege, rank, and respect when they followed rules and punishment was immediate when they broke the rules. Cadets woke up at 6am and went to bed at 10pm. In between, they were very busy, with only one hour of discretionary time each day. His self-esteem climbed, as did his motivation, ambition, and grades. A good bit of time was spent training physically, and he went from a pasty skinny kid in a dark room playing video games to a fit young man gaining 15 pounds of muscle in a year. He surrounds himself with like-minded kids on the same trajectory and is doing very well. I was unable to provide the structure he needed to flourish. At one point, I seriously thought there was a good chance he would live under a bridge one day. He has been accepted to university, and it was the Riverside Military Academy and not me who got him there.

The military school model is effective because expectations are

simple, measurable, and achievable within a defined time frame.
Achievers are promoted and transgressors are punished immediately,
fairly, and convincingly.

We should explore some elements of the military school model that
keeps kids busy and productive. Teach them the keys to success and how
to fulfill expectations in today's business culture. Rather than waste
money trying to equalize and make allowances for those unable or
unwilling to earn economic participation organically, we should
"productivise" our troubled youth.

**Start with pilot studies and find what is successful and ditch what
is not.** To stop the perpetuation of a troubled culture would take a large
shot of resources directed at a single generation, so it is best to first see if it
even works. Once people of color become the key holders of economic
participation, they can make the rules but not before. In the meantime, we
need an honest discussion over the issues. We need to rely upon the
women of the black community who are the backbone of the family
structure to make it happen. But first we need to de-corrupt the obstacles
impeding success.

Race is a classic debate between fair and unfair which both sides
complain and posture to no end. It does not matter who is right for there to
be improvement. **We are better served forgetting fair and unfair and
talking about how to improve the economic condition for people of
color in a meaningful way.** Just as important, you cannot help someone
that does not participate in the solution, so whatever game plan gets chosen
for testing needs full sign-off by all parties with a clear goal, a reasonable
time frame for success, and clear objective verifiable metrics for measuring
that success. Here is an idea worth testing:

Create an after-school program for 7-12th graders where they have a
highly-structured environment similar to the military school model. The
program would start after school and last until 9pm, for about 6 hours.
Kids would have sports, homework and tutoring, and extracurricular
activities (like personal skill lectures, discussion groups, robotics and
engineering, art, music or form a band, drama, performing rap groups....
you name it so long as it is productive). The kids would receive a meal

and head home with all their homework done.

The study needs to involve a city with a high percentage of willing participants. Again, you cannot help those that do not participate in the solution. Even though there are bound to be unwilling participants; for the sake of a clean experiment, the city might be required to pass an ordinance making participation mandatory. Kids would be evaluated based on some standard and given rank and responsibility, with reward and consequence meted out swiftly.

Let the pilot study run for 6 years to complete a full adolescent cycle before evaluating the results. The experiment needs to be thorough and not shoddy; sloppy experiments have no information value. The goal is not to be fair but to improve through experimentation with willing participants. Along the way and especially after 6 years, evaluate the grades, standardized test scores, dropout rate, job acceptance, college acceptance, crime, competency, motivation and attitudes. Evaluate the cost of the program verses the savings in social cost.

If the study fails, do not repeat. If it succeeds, do it again. In my humble little business at Mosquito Curtains, this is exactly what we do. We think an action might have a beneficial effect but such bets are always uncertain. Before laying out a ton of money with an uncertain payoff, we create mini-experiments. Many, if not most, fail despite the best prediction of a positive outcome, and that's okay. The handful of experiments that work is enough to advance with significant improvement and we pump resources into what works. We should ALWAYS be testing and stop hunching with big dollars on massive programs that always look good on paper but do not always pan out. Even if the experiment is successful, always be testing. The massive untested ubiquitous programs that fail only add fodder to negative rhetorical evaluations that encourage us to throw up our hands in frustration and spin into apathy. Tony Robbins has a slogan, "Try until." We do not give up when we teach our kids to walk. We try until they do because we have an expectation of success. Not all our coaxing and creative ideas will work to get children to walk when we want them to, but we would not think of giving up and keep trying until they do.

Will there be problems with the study I laid out? You betcha. Some kid is going to die of an overdose in the parking lot, some bus will skid off the road, and some supervisor will be prosecuted for an indiscretion. This is not utopia. It is an experiment aimed to improve.

Where will the money come from? Remember this is a relatively small study, so, State, City and Federal Governments should ALL share in the cost as a requirement. After all, they ALL have a stake in the outcome. Nonetheless, I can see business as participating with both people and resources. I can see food chains helping with meals and offering weekend jobs. I can see parent and independent-minded volunteers of all color. The required resources are used to solve a problem and there MUST be a payoff or the study must be considered a failed experiment. Should the problem be solved, resources should be tapered, just as training wheels are removed when we learn to ride a bike. Temporary improvements are of far less value than permanent improvements.

Habitat for Humanity is a fantastic program. To be eligible for a Habitat home, a person needs to volunteer 250 hours on other Habitat homes. They must take weeks of classes in personal competency so that they learn the skills to keep their home. They will eventually have a mortgage to pay for the home in order for the program to perpetuate. Other required resources, including money and volunteers are required, but the return on these dollars is astounding. Furthermore, it is an opportunity for the more affluent participants to understand the plight of someone struggling financially. Understanding creates empathy. Ask anyone who has volunteered and they will tell you it was one of the most heartening experiences they ever had.

Lastly, it breaks my heart to see what is happening in the black community amongst those within the community. I happen to own an apartment with black tenants. Something as simple as receiving mail in a mailbox can be an ordeal. Twice a month, mailboxes are looted and torn apart by those looking for scheduled checks. Whites have little to no concept of what it is like living in a tough neighborhood. As if life in a tough neighborhood is not hard enough, living paycheck to paycheck, unable to afford to stay home with a sick child, or getting around often without a car, they can't even count on their US mail delivery. Upon contacting the local post office, I could not get three phone calls returned.

Work orders were disregarded until I made clear my very white expectations. I could not, for an instant, imagine any of that happening in my own white neighborhood. And we wonder why those in the community are not like suburban soccer moms? **There is a massive misunderstanding between whites and blacks; they <u>BOTH</u> need to share life stories with each other to create MUTUAL empathy.**

They desperately need help and white suburbia is as silent as a stone thinking, "Their community, by their own people, and their problem." This is the quiet racism of indifference. It does not matter who loots the mailboxes; these good people still do not have their mail. We can kick the can down the road forever, but the only way out is through earned black economic empowerment. Blacks may not like the solution and whites may not like the solution, but there is only one solution, waiting for the day we wake up and implement it.

Education

It blows my mind how D-U-M-B we are about education and how little imagination we apply to the issue. Education is a social issue that never seems to go away. We spend a small fortune to get our kids through college and the debt incurred can burden families for many years. Some parents even deplete retirement savings to educate their kids, which creates other social problems. We are still not at full employment, yet companies complain of shortages of skilled workers in certain fields such as skilled-craftsmen.

As I had mentioned, I was a high school teacher for a year and have just a little insight. We all know a few teachers in our lives who were truly talented and made an enormous impact on our lives (bravo). We all have had incompetent teachers as well. The system is irrational. Overall, teachers are God's people; they work very hard for a pittance of a wage (unlike many European countries that value teachers more, with far better compensation). Most teachers really care. Like politics, the system that has been corrupted. We need teachers in the same way we need politicians; they just need to be led better. Some of the prescriptions described below may make teachers feel threatened. Change is always unsettling. Hopefully, all will agree that education, first, must prioritize the benefits to students. Good teachers will see their interests aligned with student interests. Bad teachers will not.

What I recall distinctly from teaching was that there were three important factors that contributed to the success of the student: the aptitude of the student, the quality of the teacher, and the home environment. Teachers had to know the material, assess student knowledge and aptitude, and then creatively guide students to learn what the course was designed to achieve. Some teachers instinctively knew how to creatively guide students from A to B and some did not. The skill seemed to be more intuitive than learned. I found that I had to first make students want to walk into my classroom and then hold their attention for an hour. If I could not do that, I was done before I started.

I was surprised to discover how important the home environment was, since it was where the EQ of the student was managed through expectation. As an idealistic teacher who knew he was only there for a year before heading off to graduate school, I made it a point to call four parents each evening to discuss their child's performance. For some, once they got over the relief that their child was not in trouble, the remainder of the phone call was just indulging a young idealistic teacher on a crusade. Many parents were terrific and very grateful but others were just plain indifferent. I concluded that it was the home environment that was a better predictor of a child's success, even over aptitude and teacher quality.

What should be the goal of our education system? **Education should be viewed as a business that produces a product at some cost.** The goal is to improve the product and reduce the cost. In many ways, we have corrupted the system with personal agendas that will be identified along the way.

I do not fully understand enough of early learning to write intelligently about grammar school. There are too many child psychology and early learning issues that I do not feel competent to speak about, so this will be limited to junior high school through college.

The Commandant at my son's high school, Marine Lt Col Kevin

Jarrard, has been a teacher for over 12 years. He explained to me the state requirement that teachers have a teaching certificate or credential. Presumably, the certificate is a measure of competency. Schools obtain accreditation, in part, based on faculty being credentialed. Private schools have more leeway, but public school teachers must be credentialed except in an emergency. To be credentialed, a person must take a series of courses and simply pass. The credential does not say whether they were outstanding in their coursework or asleep in the back of class. It does not say that the certificate holder is gifted as a speaker, charismatic, organized, competent or will be effective at shaping young minds. It does not even say that the teacher studied in the subject he or she was teaching. It merely states that they took the necessary education coursework and passed.

The Commandant went on to explain that the previous president of the school participated in two space shuttle missions, but because he was not credentialed, was not eligible to teach science in a Georgia public school without a formal exception. He had to explain to the accreditation board through a litany of listed form questions as to why the past president was not credentialed. In the end, the president continued to teach science at the school but remained a liability to the school's accreditation standing.

It seems to me that the teaching credential is not the right predictor of a person's ability to teach. What would make more sense is a knowledge exam in the field they will teach. Establish a competency review board made up of educators, parents, public speaking experts, and even some student voice. The board would affirm competency and the ability to communicate effectively. Who would not want to change the credentialed teacher policy? Bad teachers who rely on the credential to compete for jobs, supported of course by teacher unions that chose to protect them over the interests of students.

Standing in the way, would fit our definition of corruption or *the advancement of one's agenda at the imposed disadvantage of another.* A teacher's union that protects incompetence is stealing. In so far as I have ever learned, "Thou shalt not steal." **Do away with the current teaching certificate that is a senseless barrier to entry for qualified teachers.** Use competency testing and a communication skills review board as the new criteria.

Now here is where the possibilities open up. Recall that the goal is to improve the product of education and reduce cost. **Consider a triad of three teacher groups;** individuals, fresh out of college prepared to do big things in their lives, who decide to take a pit stop and teach for a year or two. The target is the best and the brightest with GPA's to prove it. They are young, motivated, and have an inspirational sparkle in their eyes.

Forget the credential that they are not inclined to work and pay for if they only plan to teach temporarily and send them through the competency board and hire the good ones. Teach for America is an example of such a program. On the other end of the spectrum, take the semi-retired, or fully retired individual like our space shuttle astronaut who is motivated to put some water back into the well. They too, are not inclined to get a credential for a temporary stint. It is a fantastic opportunity to get businesses involved that could sabbatical employees for the cause, teaching part time or full time. Send these folks through the competency board. The third group would be those wonderful core career teachers necessary to maintain continuity. They too, would go before the competency review board. The first two groups are cheap, as they are motivated more out of love for shaping young minds than they are by money. If business were involved, they could co-op with the young teachers, offering them permanent jobs after an incredibly valuable work experience. (As an aside, during my interview process at Solomon Brothers investment banking, they were as impressed with my motivation and experience to take a year off and teach as they were with my MBA from Berkeley.) From the savings in salaries, the core group of teachers could be paid more and there would still be savings.

Here is another improvement for public schools. **Make the problem smaller.** There seems to be obstruction by the school boards to allow parents to direct the education portion of tax dollars to private school tuition. A smaller problem is always easier to solve than a big one. The reason for objection is the reduction of the kingdom of influence and measurement of performance.

Public school boards are scared to death that a brain drain would hurt performance metrics, creating a public perception of incompetence. This is an easy problem to solve and I am surprised they have not done it sooner.

Metrics for state education should include both public and private schools. After all, the goal should be the overall quality of state education.

Charter schools are a fantastic example of creating isolated experiments. Charter schools have had fantastic results, and it started with an experiment that no special interest objected to, *at first*. Many of the pilot charter schools were in such trouble with few solutions that school boards were happy to oblige. It was not until charter schools began outperforming traditional public schools that conflict arose. This inconvenient truth motivated teacher unions to put pressure on politicians to call for a halt and even reverse the program.

Schools can do a much better job using technology which begs another experiment. As a math teacher, I can tell you that moving thirty kids through algebra all with different aptitudes in a subject that requires cumulative knowledge is very difficult. By the time the first semester is over, half the kids are lost and the other half are not being challenged. There are way too many great math websites and neuro-learning techniques to be stuck with the old method of lecture and spit balls. Kids can learn at a pace that suits them and learn until…they get it right.

Curriculums should be more practical and relatable to the lives of kids. A lesson in statistics is a great medium for understanding math. Currently, we teach kids about irrational numbers and 4th ordered polynomials that are great if you plan to be an engineer but entirely out of touch for the average kid and a recipe for kids to disconnect.

Technology is also a cost savings. If a teacher is going to give the same lecture year after year, which is essentially the same as all the other teachers who teach the same subject, doesn't it make sense to automate the process with a well-designed, creative and engaging, online lesson taking the best of the best lectures and let teachers fill in the gaps with lagging students?

The older the kids get; the more appropriate online work becomes. Of course, there will be those who object, perhaps math teachers. Ideas like this will be criticized for hurting jobs. **Job preservation, is NEVER a valid rationale for inefficiency.** Consider 1,000 math teachers displaced by online math courses that have proven to do a better job than the teachers themselves. You could theoretically pay the teachers to stay home, produce a better student product, and still will be better off. Perhaps the displaced teachers belong in another sector of the economy like making the next best math video or they can supplement by tutoring those that are behind.

Lastly, there is the issue of college education. **Europe has a different model for higher education.** In Europe, there are two paths for higher education. There is the university path similar to what we do here in the states and a shorter trade school path. University is a more theoretical curriculum and trade school is more practical application. When someone finishes, let's say, electrician school, they must test out to prove that they have all the necessary skills to perform a set list of tasks. Our country today has a big labor shortage in tradesmen. When a company hires an electrician in Europe, they know the abilities of the employee. Here in the states, and especially in GA, you do not know if the electrician is a NASA qualified electrician or some guy who just learned to turn a light bulb. Because trade school programs are shorter, they require less money.

I would propose a third path which is essentially a one year course on general competency. It is astounding how many people that have come into my office for a job interview and do not know what the ABC's of being a productive employee are all about. Some do not even know how to write a resume or use a spell checker. Even college kids I have hired do not seem to understand the basics of personal finance or how a mortgage works.

Similarly, just as there is a GED as a substitute for a high school diploma, there are hosts of people that have earned a life experience degree outside of college. In the extreme case consider, Bill Gates and Steve Jobs as two college dropouts. In between there are many less notables that never learned in a classroom but learned on the job. For many who have started their lives with family obligations, going back to school just is not practical nor of value. Should a Lt Col with years of leadership experience be passed over for a 21yr old with a degree in leadership? Who would you rather hire? The problem is that employers do not necessarily recognize education outside a college classroom. Since the end game of education is employment, government can lead by coopting business. Unnecessary barriers benefit the incompetent and those who certify them.

College is not for everyone, yet economic participation is painfully difficult without a college degree, although there are alternatives. Somewhere there is a disconnect between what the goal of university really is. Universities are presumably in the business of education; however, sometimes I wonder if they are in the business of issuing diplomas. We are all told we need our diplomas and need to spend lots of money getting that magic slip of paper. For me, the greatest value of college really was not the coursework or brilliant professors per se. It was being immersed in a student body, all with hopes and dreams, with a contagious ambition to do better. College is a think tank of peers. **If you put ambitious young people in a room with a common goal, with some means to measure, they will teach themselves and each other.**

Unfortunately, many online universities have not kept their promises and have soured public perception of their value. However, some offer incredible value.

Example: The world of finance is very rational and has organically created an alternative called the CFA (Chartered Financial Analyst) that has arguably exceeded the value of an MBA. The CFA is a rigorous self-study program outside the university system that focuses on practical finance and how to apply it. The program is far cheaper than an MBA and those who complete all three levels are a known commodity with known skills who can hit the ground running. In the eyes of almost all financial employers, the value of a CFA certificate outranks the MBA degree for a fraction of the cost. Ask anyone with both degrees and they will tell you that the CFA was more challenging and of greater value. This is a perfect test case that adds credence that four year theoretical degrees might not be the best value. The CFA proves that online study can work. As for many of the other online Universities, it is not the model that is bad. It is the execution that's dubious, along with the tall tales they are selling regarding value. By granulating education into theoretical and pragmatic programs within various fields, like CFA programs and trade school programs, we can create a better product for far less money.

Lastly, we need to have an expectation on students who use

government funding to complete an education. If commerce needs more chemical engineers and no more sculptors, why are resources available equally? This does not suggest that sculpting is not important but is a luxury we can't afford equally to need. The arts are important and worthy endeavors for the cultural development of our society, but we must prioritize correctly, particularly when resources are limited. Better yet, a trade school for sculpting can justify the lower cost of producing sculptors. Why must they usurp resources from disadvantaged kids, who may really need economically viable skills?

It kills me when some use grants and scholarships with no intention of entering the work force. As you will see in a later chapter, I am squarely behind the empowerment of women. But one woman who uses government resources to become a sophisticated stay-at-home mom should not usurp the resources that could be used by another woman trying to make a career for herself (further empowering women). As a society, we must eat first and then explore what is higher on Maslow's pyramid, especially when resources are limited.

Politicians are lost and leadership is conspicuously absent and they measure by budget size. One party argues, "We need education more accessible to all through MORE funding." While from the other side of the aisle, "It is fiscally irresponsible to go into debt for another social program." The answer is a smarter and cheaper education system that produces a better product.

Teachers are a powerful voice. In GA, they managed to tip the scales and voted out an incumbent Governor who challenged the system. Bad teachers certainly do not want the rules to change; the good ones should. But we need to understand the goal of education. Is the goal smarter, cheaper education that produces a better product or is it job security for teachers? We can do either but we can't have both.

Nature Corruption

The main purpose for bringing up this issue is to demonstrate that one's inherent nature in and of itself cannot be considered corruption. This topic of Gay rights seems to always come up on the campaign trail. I suppose if you feel that homosexuality is a lifestyle choice for otherwise straight people and a violation against God's law, it would make sense to be against gay rights. If you felt that gays had a high propensity to molest children then they should be prohibited from adopting kids. From this camp, homosexuals are corrupting us and the discussion is over.

Unfortunately, every credible scientific study indicates that while homosexuality is not normal, it is natural. Gays do not choose to be gay and to voluntarily subject themselves to the harshness society subjects upon them, any more than I would choose to hammer my thumb. Gay men have proven to have no more of a propensity to molest minors than straight men.

What is inherent to a human being is not and cannot be corrupt in and of itself. A black person is inherently black; a woman is inherently a woman. Any attempt to restrict the rights of an individual by virtue of their inherent nature is corrupt.

Homosexuals can't wish themselves straight any more than I can wish myself an Italian trapeze artist. To exclude homosexuals from the full rights as citizens because of inherent identity traits is corrupt. Doing so would open the door to exclude the inherent nature of any citizen society deemed to be different. This has been done before and we consider those events barbaric. Those that exclude the inherent nature of an individual will eventually find themselves on the wrong side of history.

Immigration

Our current illegal Mexican immigration problem demonstrates how corruption of foreign governments steals from US Citizens. Mexico is rich in natural resources and has talented hard-working citizenry. On paper, it has every reason to flourish. If you want a great example of what runaway corruption can do, just look across the border. There is a small privileged class and everybody else. From politicians, government contractors, judges, narcos, and all the way down to the policeman with a gun and the postal system, corruption is more the norm than the exception in Mexico.

From a Mexican heritage, myself, I can tell you that there is a caste system. Privilege is so deeply engrained that it is even seen in the conjugation of verbs. Carlos Salinas was a president who was heralded for cleaning up the excesses of corruption and modernizing Mexico. When he left office, he is reported to have stolen hundreds of millions of dollars and stashed in various accounts around the world, some of which was discovered and returned to Mexico. He managed to retain enough stolen booty to live a very comfortable life in Dublin, Ireland.

The ultimate reason for Mexicans fleeing to America is the lack of opportunity and security for those disenfranchised by corruption. If the United States did not facilitate Mexican corruption, it would be a great first step to curbing illegal immigration. If we went a step further and attacked Mexican corruption, there would be no illegal immigration. But do we really have the moral authority since people in glass houses should not throw stones? First, we need to clean our own house and lead by example in a wave that just might be contagious.

The issue of immigration is a function of which group entity we are solving for. Are we solving as a global group or a national group? Are we citizens of the planet or of America?

Recall that we are born unequally and I have made arguments against equalization as a viable strategy. When it comes to foreigners, our only obligation is to not corrupt foreign entities. It would be compassionate to help out, but we are not obliged so long as we did not corrupt their circumstance. You can only help those that participate in the solution. America cannot be a dumping ground for those avoiding the fundamental corruption that drives Mexican families to the United States. We are far better served to not enable Mexican corruption and to aid in the end of Mexican corruption wherever we can. Mexicans must be the front line of their own battles. If we become the relief valve, the stress level to the disenfranchised Mexican group entity never hits a high enough level to effect change.

Unfortunately, illegal immigration imposes the consequences of corrupt Mexican governance on Americans. To my knowledge, the United States has done absolutely nothing to curb Mexican government corruption. In the meantime, we have a right to decide who enters our country and to define a real border. For those 13 million who are already here, we must seriously enact some practical immigration reform. If illegal immigrants are not productive contributors of value, they should be asked to leave.

For those who are contributors of value, there needs to be some path to citizenship. We must abandon ideology that does not serve us. Rule of law is critical in any society. Unfortunately, it has gone on for generations and we now need to be pragmatic. Had we had comprehensive housing, employment, and birth citizenship laws, there would have been absolutely no benefit to crossing the border. Frankly it is just too late to turn back the clock and to do it differently. We have a de facto situation and the same rationale for statutes of limitation applies. We screwed up; we can't go back in time and undo the new lives, legal or not, that have been established. Now we need to do it differently. To get hung up on the violation of rule of bad law just does not make sense when those laws were just plain inadequate to begin with. We need to get real with ourselves. We are not about to barge into homes and drag families out who have been washing our dishes, picking our produce and, cleaning our toilets for the past 30 years. By getting hung up on "bad rule of law" when it has been so inadequate for so long, may play well to a conservative's constituency back home, but it is just getting in the way of a realistic solution.

Let me say, most these people are hardworking people who have taken jobs we do not want. They can't be faulted and should not be demonized for trying to make a better life for their families. They deserve dignity. If your family was suffering, would you let a border stop you if you lived under the same corrupt conditions, danger, and lack of opportunity? Compassionate societies have earned moral authority which is invaluable. **Compassionate societies flourish.** We need to enact immigration reform, but with dignity and respect or else we have no moral authority to assume a leadership role in the world. Compassion is harmoniously congruous with leadership. We need a consensus approach that is fair, equitable and reaffirms self-reliance.

D. Income & Wealth Inequality

The Rich need the Poor to be Rich

Imagine this scenario: Bill Gates, Ted Turner, Donald Trump, the Koch Brothers, Mark Cuban and Warren Buffet are all stranded on a deserted Island with an ATM giving them access to all their wealth. Who is going to cook the meals, press the suits, or clean the commode? They certainly could not pay each other enough to perform these tasks. As a small business owner, I fully understand and appreciate the symbiotic relationship I have with my employees. I would be short-sighted to take the exclusive attitude that they would not have a job if it were not for me. The fact is that I would not have a business if it were not for them.

I have 20 employees that work in my business at Mosquito Curtains and I spend time speaking to each one of them. I explain that I pay them $16/hr because I charge $30 for what I expect to equal an hour of their work. The more value they can produce in that hour, the more money I make, plain and simple. The harder they work, the easier it is for me to pay for my life. I go on to explain to them that my least expensive and most valuable employee makes $20/hr because he can sew like a maniac. I had to pay him more than anyone else or some other employer would. Furthermore, I needed to demonstrate to all employees that their productivity mattered. What gives me the right to make money from their labor? I risked my capital, sweated my blood, and used my creativity to create an opportunity that they could not create for themselves. The market rate in GA for their skills is $10/hour, so I am easily able to attract their talent. They are not chained to their desk and are free to leave any time they choose to find a better opportunity. I expect that if and when they can, they will do so unless I am able to continue providing an incentive to stay. In no way are they coerced to stay. We need each other for our respective roles.

On a trip to Lima, Peru, I marveled at how inexpensive it was to live there. The climate was very similar to that of Southern California and our host had a top floor condominium, a country club membership, and another condo at the beach, all for what a middle-class retirement could afford.

Then I saw why. The indigenous people did all the work for a pittance of a wage. When the working class gets seriously sick, they die. Without taking any position on the equity of the situation, it appears very clear that the rich need the poor to be rich. There is no way on earth that a middle-class retiree could live such a lifestyle unless there were people willing to work for $1.75/hr. This is just a fact. We should appreciate those out there who through their own circumstance, uncorrupted by others, have no better opportunity than to work at wages that enable our lifestyles. We do not owe more than a free market wage, though we should appreciate them for what they do for us and not stand in the way of their achieving a better life through quiet collusion. If we were to go a step further, we might recognize that we capitalists would not have what we have if it were not for the labor of the *working man*. When the disparity gets too far out of hand, perhaps we owe them something and should put a little water back into the well. We do not have to, but remember, they can vote too.

Within Obama Care was a universal healthcare premise. Should every working American have the right to healthcare? But wait a minute. Is that consistent with a free market? Since we are not really corrupting his ability to earn a living, we really have no obligation under the corruption definition to do anything, right?

We make the rules and we can take a compassionate route and say that if the guy cleaning our toilets gets diabetes and can't afford to buy insulin that we should collectively pitch in and help through universal healthcare. Alternatively, we can say, "too bad", he could have gone to college and made a better life for himself. Had he made the right life decisions, he could have afforded his own insulin. Let him die and just get another toilet cleaner from the unemployment pool. But if we make the decision to treat toilet cleaners like disposable razors, we should have the guts to step forward and just say so. If it is okay to do it, then why not be transparent about it. The KKK wore hoods because it was not okay.

I find it remarkable that those opposed to universal healthcare are unwilling to step forward and honestly say to the toilet cleaners, "If you get sick, you will probably die, and I'm sorry but we will do nothing to save you." For Sean Hannity to say that all toilet cleaners should go to college like he did so that they can afford to get sick, just is not realistic. After all, who would clean our toilets? If the rich are to be rich, we need high school drop outs and those unable to get their lives together for whatever reason to have a better opportunity than to earn a crap wage. But it needs to be a living wage or they will not live. The rich need the poor to be rich. The capitalist class needs the working class to become rich and needs the working class to enjoy the wealth.

Once again, forget morality for a moment. **Is it in the interest of the rich to be compassionate?** Remember that money and people equal influence. Money can only be used to persuade people, but in the end, people vote, and form groups of rebellion. Remember, Italian citizens were the ones who hung Mussolini from a gas station. The rich have lots of money but are relatively few in number. We would not be talking about class warfare if the working class did not feel disenfranchised. The liberal great society would have no advocates if the working class felt things were going swimmingly. If the rich do not follow the harmony of the road, there will be repercussions in the form of the masses voting for Robin Hood laws. People with little to lose become desperate and desperate people can be dangerous voters. In the softest sense, they can act out politically. In the most severe case, they can act out criminally or act out against other family members though emotional and physical abuse that diminishes our society.

In countries where there is a huge gap between rich and poor, the rich live behind high walls and barbed wire fences. To an outside observer, the rich live in fancy golden prisons with armed guards because they do not feel safe. Forget morality and what is right and wrong; it is in the interest of the rich to be compassionate.

Dan Ariely, in a TED Talk posed the following question. If you divide the American public into 5 equal buckets, what would you guess is the percentage of wealth held by each bucket? The respondents guessed that the lowest 20% (A) held 2.9% of the wealth, the next bucket (B) held 6.4%, (C) = 12%, (D) = 20.2% and the top 20% (E) held 58.5% of the wealth.

Then they were asked what the distribution should be such that if they were randomly placed in any of the 5 buckets (like at birth) that they would be indifferent. A = 10.5%, B=14.1%, C=21.4%, D=22% and the top group, E = 33%. Surprisingly, the answers were all very similar across wealth, nationality, gender, and even similar between conservatives and liberals. The conclusion is that respondents felt we were not as balanced in wealth as they would like to be in a fair society such that they would be indifferent if randomly placed in any bucket.

There was a very surprising difference between what people felt to be the current distribution of wealth and what they felt to be a fair distribution of wealth. Keep in mind that the answers were all surprisingly similar across several demographics. Now the big shocker was to look at the actual distribution of wealth where A = 0.1%, B=0.2%, C=3.9%, D=11.3%, and E=84.4%. The conclusion is that our ideal for wealth distribution is not as balanced as we thought we were. Our intuition of current income equality is far from factual. Our ideal balance for equality is enormously different than the actual state of wealth distribution. Why is there such disparity between intuition, sense of fairness, and the facts?

	Guess at Distribution	Ideal State	Actual State
(E) Top 20%	58.5%	33.0%	84.4%
(D) Second Top 20%	20.0%	22.0%	11.3%
(C) Middle 20%	12.0%	21.4%	3.9%
(B) Second bottom 20%	6.4%	14.1%	0.2%
(A) Bottom 20%	2.9%	10.5%	0.1%

The Poor Need The Rich To Allocate Capital

Conversely, the wealthy capitalist class provides a critical benefit to the working class. Wealth from legitimate profit means that the capitalist has invested in a viable business because profit validates an economic effort. The role of capital allocator is critical within any economy and this fact is often missed by those eager to demonize the rich. Capital allocators take risk and deploy capital in worthy economic investments that ultimately provide productive jobs for the working class. If a business is sustainable, it is profitable and will live on, continuing to employ workers. A bad allocation of capital wastes time and otherwise productive resources tantamount to throwing money down the drain.

A capitalist can do three things with wealth: (1) reinvest his capital to grow a business or perhaps create a new business; (2) give the money to charity, or (3) can spend the money on consumption. With respect to reinvestment and charity, he is providing a benefit to the working class by either creating another job or by voluntarily sharing his wealth back to the working class.

Successful capitalists are not villains of our society; they are heroes, especially when they create more value than they consume. **We wrongly target the rich for the sake of being rich.** These are wise allocators of capital and critical to the advancement of civilization. The corrupt are the villains in society. Not all wealthy people are corrupt though some corrupt people are rich. It would be shooting ourselves in the foot to simply address income inequality based on wealth alone. For the value capitalist who is innovating and allocating capital efficiently and honestly, bravo, keep doing what you are doing and thank you. You can take the bull's eye off your forehead by joining the fight against corrupt acquirers of wealth who are the real villains.

Free Markets

Free markets work and history seems to have proven that anytime someone monkeys with the free market, something goes terribly wrong. A free market transaction occurs when someone voluntarily parts with cash in their wallet for some value they find in a good or service. Free markets are not subsidized transactions and they are not forced or dishonestly influenced in any way. The price of goods and services is determined by how much money people are willing to exchange for those goods and services. Prices self-adjust based on the laws of supply and demand and free market transactions are entirely rational. **Profit validates a free market activity.** Without profit, a private business is unsustainable.

The old Soviet Union had a command economy whereby the government decided what everyone needed and set production quotas to fill those needs. Many if not most of the prices were controlled. The result was that Soviets only received goods and services that were planned for them by the command economy; they had no choice. The outcome was often great shortages or great surpluses when the government's estimates did not match the desires of the citizens. The economic plan was a complete failure and most communist countries have abandoned a centrally planned economy. **One of the biggest problems in any economy is that markets are not free enough**.

Many problems we have faced in the past are the result of government meddling with free markets. The prelude to the financial crisis was a liberal movement to make housing more affordable by relaxing lending standards. As a consequence, people who could not really afford to buy a house were purchasing homes that they were unable to afford. Financial institutions got into the game and stretched the rules of lending to its limit with deception, delusion, and loop holes. Subsequently, a cool wind blew and the house of cards came tumbling down.

We have allowed some subsidies that are a huge violation of free market principles and that artificially changed our behavior. Why do we subsidize corn? Corn is artificially cheap and is fed to cattle so that we purchase meat at the grocery store far less than it would be under free market conditions. Sounds like a great idea, right? We need protein and what better source of protein than a fat juicy cut of beef. Subsidizing corn saves the family farm and makes meat far cheaper at the grocery store (some argue nine times cheaper than it would be in an unsubsidized market). What could possibly be wrong with that? Oh yeah, and everybody needs milk, right?

Credible studies show that meat and dairy are not the wonder foods we have been led to believe. Meat and dairy are huge contributors to heart disease and cancer. As much as I love a good steak, touting that these food groups are essential to our diets is a myth. After age 24, when our bodies and brains are fully developed, meat and dairy is not in the best interest of our health. Populations with the greatest longevity have very low consumption of meat and dairy products. As it turns out, fruits and vegetables are far more nutritious and less harmful to both our health and health care costs. I would strongly encourage watching the films "Forks Over Knives" and "Food Inc", which are on Netflix and both worth watching to form your own opinion. President Clinton quietly subscribes to these diets and is largely the reason why Uncle Billy is not so large anymore after his heart surgery.

Any time we interfere with free markets by using subsidies, we corrupt profit as the true validator of an economic effort. The only valid reason for a subsidy or targeted economic tax would be to compensate for externalities.

An externality is a consequence of an economic activity that is experienced by unrelated third parties. An externality can be either positive or negative. For example, a factory that dumps waste water in a river creates a negative externality for anyone using the river. Sending a rocket into space is a positive externality by creating the technology that can be used to launch a communication satellite. Free markets do not always account for externalities. Regulation and subsidies presumably try to adjust for externalities. Regulation against negative externalities is an ongoing effort; however, subsidies to promote positive externalities must be temporary and measurable. Unless there is an eventual free market profit to validate an economic effort, economic subsidies make no sense whatsoever. The system of subsidies has been corrupted and needs a serious re-evaluation. Why do we subsidize mortgage interest with a tax write off? Sure, I love my mortgage deduction, but fundamentally why do I deserve it? What limited positive externality is it creating? Why am I subsidized and the guy in the apartment is not? Why would I be even more subsidized by buying a bigger house?

Owning a home has some positive externality in that neighborhoods with a higher percentage of home ownership tend to have safer and cleaner neighborhoods. Homeowners simply care more about protecting an environment where they are financially vested. But there is a limit to this positive externality and there should be a limit to the mortgage interest deduction that subsidizes this positive externality. Home mortgage subsidies above the limit to its positive externality (like the median home price) are not in place to create positive externalities. They are in place because they are popular and tampering with popular perks gets a politician unelected. Mortgages are big money to financial institutions.

What is the true cost of oil? Oil is a national treasure. As I mentioned earlier, it takes millions of years to whip up another batch. No royalty is paid for the depletion of a finite national treasure. If you control the land, you own the oil. In fact, since 1913, there were substantial tax incentives for drilling oil through the oil depletion allowance. Doing so in 1913, may have made sense, but in 2020, it does not, especially since we have a greater understanding just how finite this resource is.

Consider the negative externalities of oil. For me to drive my car, I pollute the air. Who pays for that? We spent over a trillion dollars to protect our oil interest in the Middle East. Who pays for that? **Unless we allocate true costs and assign them to where they belong, we make bad economic decisions.** A laissez-faire attitude that ignores true cost because someone got away without paying for a negative externality is not a free market. Currently, alternative energy such as wind, solar, geothermal, and alternative biofuels (e.g. ethanol, also subsidized) do not compare economically to oil-based fuel. However, if the true cost of oil were assigned to prices, alternative energy certainly would start to make more sense. We are making bad economic decisions because we do not account for externalities and we disrupt the free market with popular subsidies; it is corporate welfare.

Back in the days of Gyork, humans discovered they had different skill sets. Specialization occurred and trading began in a barter system. I will make you a chair if you give me five chickens. Before too long, bartering was just too cumbersome. I need chickens but the guy raising chickens needs seed and I do not have seed and he does not want a chair. So, I walk to the fellow who makes seed and talk him into buying a chair so that I can trade his seeds for chickens.

Early man came up with a currency. At first the currency was probably some commodity everybody used and was a good medium for trading, like beads or metals. Over the years, currency has evolved to what it is today. Presumably, currency is a representation of value. I sell mosquito curtains as an alternative to a screen porch. I may sell a curtain *system for $800 in a free market transaction. I deliver my client's curtain and she pays me $800 that represents the value she deems I have created. The currency transaction is just an accounting entry. I now have $800 that represents the value I have created. She now has a new mosquito curtain with $800 less buying potential. The currency enables me to exchange that value for something I may want now or in the future.*

Now here is a major point. **Value is not necessarily required to get the script we call currency.** Value does not buy goods and services; currency buys goods and services. No one asks where I got the money when selling me something. I could have earned it, found it, stole it, or cheated someone for it. The vendor only cares that I have the money to pay for what he is selling. Our economic endeavors have become less about the value and more about the money, which is supposed to but does not necessarily represent value.

The biggest problem I have is that many transactions are not free market transactions. Consider executive pay that tends to be more of a collusive transaction than a free market transaction. I have seen firsthand that, in all the public corporations I have ever worked for, there is a boy's club at the top. The boy's club's primary motivation is to pay themselves as much as possible, while offering shareholders a respectable return and paying the worker bees just enough to man their post. The boy's club has a handful of people at the top, buffered by a loyal second tier who are paid to support them, followed by a third tier who will do anything it takes to one day become full members of the boy's club. How is compensation determined? Is it a free market transaction or are the rules collusively set by the boy's club? When time comes to find another board director, will that person be an executive compensation miser or a friend known for executive philanthropy? The most reliable board member is another CEO whose board the executive sits on reciprocally.

The S&P 500 is littered with examples of CEO's who have given mediocre performance and were politely allowed to resign with huge severance packages. In Atlanta, one executive had a very mediocre performance, yet managed a quarter billion compensation exit package as he walked out the door. He went to head yet another firm, did a mediocre job for two years and walked away with another $50MM. He was a man whose wealth was not representative of his value contribution since he managed to legally rig the system. He thought the money was his to keep and forgot that it was shareholder money. He had a fiduciary responsibility to be a good custodian and by no means steal it.

At a cocktail party, I brought this up. One man lauded the Atlanta executive as a Lion. "He legally worked the system to his advantage, he made a lot of money for his family, and he's a hero in my book." Now this man happened to think Obama was a shameless redistributor of wealth, so I responded to him. "Guess what? Obama thinks he's a Lion, too. He's targeting Mr. Atlanta and everyone else with money, including you. This jackass just contributed to Obama's argument and empowered exactly what you do not want to happen."

Even politicians focus on the cash and not on the value contribution that the cash is supposed to represent. **Unfortunately, we do not go after the corruptors of value. Instead, we take the wrong course of action and try to redistribute wealth.** When we, as a society, have a disparity between wealth and true value-added, we would rather focus on the wealth and not on the value. This is one reason why we get into discussions of wealth redistribution instead of attacking the real problem. Wealth redistribution is bad for everyone. Legitimately earned wealth should be celebrated. We attack wealth because we have lost faith in our ability to make markets freer and have come to accept corruption as a way of life. We attack all wealth because we are lazy and are suspicious that all wealth is corrupt when in fact nothing could be further from the truth.

I would not have the slightest objection to private companies paying executives whatever they like. They are not publicly traded and are only accountable to their employees, who are free to leave. But a publicly traded company has a primary responsibility to the shareholders, who are ultimately the investing public. If something smells fishy, it is.

The rules set by these executive pay packages are often based purposely on short term targets. Executives can easily manipulate the metrics that determine short term compensation at the expense of future years. It can be subtle or blatant and there is tremendous leeway.

A perfect example is the Wells Fargo case of cross selling services. Someone in upper management decided to pressure low level bank employees to open multiple accounts for clients. Quotas were established and threats of termination were so threatening that bank employees started opening multiple accounts for clients without their permission and coming in on weekends without pay to do so. The targets were published in the annual report and the stock price loved it. Yet when revealed how they went about it, the CEO decided to fire the low-level bank employees. Elizabeth Warren eviscerated the CEO during a hearing, suggesting that the firings were the most gutless cowardly thing for him to do and that the boost in his personal wealth during the malfeasance period, amounting to over $200MM, should be returned. Nonetheless, he will likely get away with it and keep his unearned fraud-induced compensation. The episode never would have happened had the CEO been compensated on long term performance, or had to pay treble damages, or if we enacted laws with "claw-back" provisions.

CEO's of public firms often have an exaggerated sense of contribution. They can claim disproportionate responsibility for success as if the 40,000 other employees had nothing to do with it. They can be quick to blame others when things go poorly, insulating themselves from scrutiny. Becoming CEO requires ambition, an ability to navigate corporate politics, some good fortune, and presumably achievement; however, CEOs often confuse the political prowess it took to become CEO with true value-added as CEO. To beat the enormous odds and simply become CEO sometimes instills an arrogant sense of entitlement, regardless of performance. This legacy has shaped expectations that CEOs of public companies should earn obscene amounts of money that do not necessarily correlate with value contribution.

Ever see a merger occur where the acquired executives were not guaranteed a position in the new boy's club with guaranteed compensation. If you have, it was because they either got paid off with golden parachutes or the deal did not happen. Shareholders do not make mergers happen, executives do. Shareholders are an afterthought. The acquiring firm knows what it really takes to get the green light and they pay off the right people to make it happen.

With every form of corruption there is generally deliberate lack of transparency. Do we even know what these guys make? The formulas and reporting are so convoluted that it takes an equity analyst to figure it out. Believe me, there is more behind the scenes than what the average Joe can cipher in the annual report. The problem with executive compensation is that it is not subject to the free market and is not transparent. Executive compensation breeds class resentment when it is not fairly earned at the expense of shareholders who are bearing the risk as investors and employees turning the hamster wheel. It is classic corruption and encourages others to cheat. The scary news is that cheating free-market compensation principles is perfectly legal.

Executives manipulating the loopholes of this flawed system are law abiding citizens. They, by their example encourage others to corrupt. All John T. Public knows is that there is another poster boy who has managed to cheat the system who is very rich. Mr. Public might make the leap that all wealth is illegitimate and rationalize that wealth redistribution would be a fair remedy; however, such a remedy creates collateral damage to those who fairly earned wealth.

It would behoove wealthy, genuine adders of value, to go after the scoundrels who have cheated the system lest they be lumped into the same group. As previously discussed regarding race, if you do not want to be profiled, either do not fit the pattern or go after those who are creating the wrong perceptions. **Genuine adders of value should be lauded as the great contributors of society.** Wealth that is truly earned is good in a free market, and the more the better. Undeserved redistribution of wealth is wrong at ALL levels. Executive siphoning of money from the public has rippling effects, dare I say down to crime in the streets. Corruptors of value should be stopped with better rules and jailed if they violate those rules. Financial envy flourishes, particularly when wealth is construed to be unearned. When wealth does not clearly and accurately represent contribution of value, the door is open to envy, resentment, and the spawning of more cheaters. When others trust in the accounting system in which wealth is determined by contribution of real value, I suspect that resentment is, in part, replaced with respect.

Free market corruption happens on both ends of the spectrum. The welfare recipient who has lied on the application and uses the money to go on a cruise is just as much of a scoundrel as the CEO who manipulates his compensation outside the free market. However, the impact of the one CEO can exceed the impact of a thousand fraudulent welfare cases.

Wide swaths of corruption are entirely legal under our current set of laws. The income gap that has spawned class warfare is a rich verses poor issue; however, it is the wrong issue. The Liberal solution is a Robin Hood solution equalizing through taxation. Such methods are misguided since it targets the wrong people. The Conservative view is to protect wealth regardless of whether it was obtained by contribution or corruption, so long as it was obtained legally. The real war should be between the contributors and the corruptors of value and they are not confined to class. By focusing on an accurate accounting of value, the income gap will close on its own.

Lastly, regulation is a double edge sword that can either stop or support corruption. Despite political rhetoric, regulation is neither all good nor all bad. Many would have us believe that regulation always undermines the free market, and in some cases, it does. However, in many cases, regulation actually promotes a free market by checking corruptors and by assigning negative externality costs that are impossible to account without regulation.

Value Based Employment

Value based employment is simply productive employment at a fair market wage dictated by a free market. We focus on employment statistics such as the number of jobs created in a month and those filing for unemployment. But the quality of those jobs and the value-added are what is important.

To impress a beautiful cave girl, Gyork was inspired to create a magic machine that would do all the work in the village to fulfill the needs of all 100 cave dwellers. The machine was ingenious and could be operated by just one man. Gyork presented his new machine to the cave dweller council. Since Gyork invented the machine he felt it was his right to have all its benefits. Because the other cave dwellers no longer had to work the fields, Gyork felt they should build him a castle and should serve him. The response was a big fat NO! So Gyork offered to donate the machine to the community.

Unfortunately, they thought it was now the second dumbest idea any cave dweller ever came up with. They argued that the unemployment rate would sky rocket from 2% to 99%. Besides, who would have to work the machine? Gyork scratched his head, then suggested the cave dwellers hold a lottery for who would work the machine each month while ninety-nine cave dwellers enjoyed a life of leisure. The cave dweller union bosses and businesses owners convinced the cave dwellers that it was a bad idea and they tossed Gyork's machine into a ravine. Everyone went back to work.

Every week we hear politicians nix ideas for efficiency because it will hurt jobs. More accurately, they will hurt the politician's ability to boast job creation. We could eliminate unemployment tomorrow by outlawing street sweeping machines and hiring the unemployed to clean streets with tooth brushes, but it would not create a value-added job.

Unions are advocates for labor but not for efficient commerce. They have a power base and sometimes undermine value employment. Hostess had two delivery unions: one that delivered cakes and one that delivered bread to the same stores, duplicating routes. Two trucks from Hostess had to deliver goods to the exact same stores. The company was in serious financial trouble and desperately needed to consolidate routes to cut costs. Since it would cause layoffs, the unions refused to allow a driver to deliver more than one category of product. Also, a Twinkie loader was not allowed to load bread even on a bread truck. Hostess went belly up because it was no longer viable and all delivery drivers were dismissed. Bravo to the unions who had just negotiated their workers out of a job. Be careful what you ask for, because you just might get it.

Similarly, the city council of Santa Monica had the bright idea to pass an ordinance forbidding banks to charge an ATM service fee to clients of other banks. Guess how many ATMs there were in Santa Monica in the months to follow? You guessed it. The city council quietly rescinded the ordinance and the banks reopened the ATMs.

Full "value employment" should be the goal of our economy. Unions obstructing efficiency for the sake of jobs, it is always wrong by corrupting the free market. Collective bargaining for a fair wage and working conditions is one thing but contriving inefficiency for the sake of jobs not rational, especially when such actions cross the threshold of economic viability. What we do with the unemployed is an entirely different issue.

The cave dweller's dilemma of what to do with Gyork's fancy machine is critical. As we displace workers with rational technology, we need to re-evaluate who owns the machine. There will always be friction between labor saving technology and labor.

Government's economic goal should be to promote productive value jobs for everyone who needs one. Who needs a job? Everyone with bills to pay and does not have enough wealth to sustain them. The jobs need to be productive and not forced on commerce for number count. We spoke of labor shortages in certain fields. As I write this, there are labor unions stuffing jobs while we have a shortage of skilled tradesmen.

Government tends to be backwards when it comes to jobs. When tax revenues are high, government buys goods and services that only bid up the cost of labor. It seems to make sense in this case to pay as you go, but it really does not; capitalism is cyclical. High unemployment periods are the right time to invest in public infrastructure and keep our workforce productive. When the economy is hot and unemployment is low, government should not compete with private industry for labor and save infrastructure projects for a rainy day. The problem is EQ. We do not have the discipline. Politicians have no sense of timing and will do anything to turn on the gas in any environment. Government should think of itself as a business, where timing is everything.

The role of government with respect to capitalism is to maintain full value-added employment. It is quite a challenge to encourage both technology and rationality while maintaining full employment.

E. Government Money In & Money Out

Government should manage its budget like a family would by accumulating wealth during good times and dipping into savings on the rainy days when needed. Similar to the way the Federal Reserve turns the interest rate knobs to raise and lower the heat in our economy, we might try a variable component of taxation whereby tax rates rise in a heated economy and fall in a weak economic cycle. Unfortunately, government suffers from low EQ and the group entity of government, in its own life drama, has a natural drive to push the boundaries of stress. Political group entity continues with bad behavior even though we can all see that it would not be sustainable. When the economy is roaring and we have an opportunity to save or pay down debt to be used later on a rainy day.

The United States had relatively little debt until the Great Depression and WWII. Implementing FDR's Great Society was absolutely necessary at the time as we were in a world of hurt. Unfortunate during what seemed to be the boom years of the Roaring Twenties we never socked away a little money away for what was to come later. After all, we had experienced 47 Recessions and 4 Economic Depressions since 1790. During those downturns, Americans just suffered, but the Great Depression of the early 30's was a different animal. Rather than being proactive early, we could only be reactive when it was too late; a low EQ trait similar to the kids in the room craving doughnuts. Large group entities hate short term pain, even if it is not in their long-term interest.

Fast forward to today and we have debt levels that question sustainability. Some of the talking heads even minimize the overall impact, arguing that debt is a normal occurrence in any business and is perfectly acceptable. As a business owner myself, I chose the path of zero debt. At any opportunity, I paid down all personal debt. When my business accumulates cash, I even go as far as to prepay future obligations such as rent and taxes, or purchase inventory I anticipate needing. Taking this path is a very conservative way to run a business, but it is safe and I can handle almost any imponderable without going belly up. I am responsible for the livelihoods of 20 employees and consider it a fiduciary responsibility to keep them safe.

Accumulated wealth is power. **The United States has far more practical influence with its purse than it will ever have with its army.** Wealth is comparable to a fully charged battery with potential, while debt depletes the battery's potential. The Iraq Wars are a classic example of a Sun Tzu principle in that war weakens both participants. One could argue the necessity of the two Gulf Wars, but, regardless of your position, the war weakened the United States financially. All wars do. When the opportunity to broaden global democracy during the Arab Spring arose, our battery was depleted and we were forced to stay on the sidelines. A huge opportunity to lessen global corruption through democratization simply passed us by. Both Russia and China have recognized our depleted resources and are challenging us for global position.

Government has never had the burden of making a profit that private business has. The only constraint that government has is a budget. Profit validates any economic effort. Politicians speak about dollars devoted to worthy causes such as ensuring school kids get a lunch each day, but they never speak of how many kids who might ordinarily not eat lunch are now eating lunch and at what cost. They do not speak about the quality of that lunch or any of the other metrics. For all we know the kids are eating potato chips and sodas. This all sounds good and the dollars are impressive but, what if the kids really need coats, or books, or a solution to that abusive father who drinks away family resources. That is not to say that these are not worthy causes for which we should devote public resources, but privatization and rigorous measurement metrics seems to be the better course of action than the randomness of a government budget.

Government procurement is highly bureaucratic and non-competitive. To create fairness amongst vendors and to prevent the likelihood of being charged $20,000 for a hammer, the government instituted rules for procurement. Our solution was to spend $3 on bureaucracy to prevent $1 of abuse. The hands of procurement officers are tied and they cannot purchase the best products and services at the best price. Small business is precluded from many government contracts because they do not have the resources to sift through the bureaucracy. Here is a great example.

As a small business owner, I was told that the only way to really see government contracts is to get placed on a preapproved vendor list called the Government Services Administration (GSA) schedule. It is so difficult to get listed that an entire cottage industry has developed to help companies to get on to the schedule. The process is so complicated that, for about $5,000, these professionals will "try" to get you listed, but with no promises. In so many cases, I have to pass on government business because I just do not have the resources to sift through the bureaucracy.

As a small business owner, I am ineligible to compete on price and merit. Government budgets are notorious for padding. Occasionally, we do business with government entities who stuff purchases at the end of their budget cycle. The way government budgets work is that if you do not use it, you lose it for next year's budget. There is an opportunity for proxy-profit. Recall the budget sequester that required government entities to take a 10% across the board cut? Remember we were told that all hell would break loose? It was amazing how the government entities absorbed the cuts barely noticeable to Joe citizen. It makes you wonder just how inefficient they have been all these years.

We need to end the *use it or lose it* budget mentality of government as a participant in commerce. Here's an idea. If a government entity were to spend $1MM less than budgeted, let the next year's budget decline by half of the savings ($500k) and reward the entity for the savings with a onetime 20% performance bonus, provided they could maintain the quality of service mandated. That's right, pay a $200k bonus to employees at a government entity. If individuals within the entity find a way to willfully cheat the system for personal gain, they are thieves and must repay triple what they have stolen. Work out the math and the tax payer wins.

Our economy should be privatized as much as possible since the government economy is not bound in any way to free market principles. Do not be shy about introducing a bonus pool for coming under budget, with strict metrics on performance to ensure that services are being delivered. The more a government entity behaves like a for-profit business, the more rational, efficient, and beneficial to tax payers. We simply need to apply appropriate metrics to ensure we are still receiving our targeted deliverable.

Transparency is a huge problem with respect to how we report government accounting. Even the unscrupulous Enron executives would have blushed if they had used the same accounting methods used by the U.S. Government. California Governor Jerry Brown proclaimed that he had balanced the budget in California. One would assume that tax revenues covered state outlays, right? Californians were not so lucky, as the state sold large chunks of public land and issued a bond to make up for the shortfall. Yet, according to Uncle Jerry and fuzzy accounting, California is in the "black". It is impossible to sustain!

Lastly, stop shifting funds between government accounts. If money is not used the way it was designated, it needs to go back to the Treasury and nowhere else. Legislation will be required to close this often-used loop hole to misappropriate funds. If the money is not being used in one area and is needed in another, fine. Just go through the process of re-legislating funds and make it transparent.

Social Security

The largest component of our debt is Social Security and Medicare. Social Security was enacted under FDR in 1935 and Medicare was added by Lyndon Johnson in 1966. Both are noble causes though they are simply unsustainable. **Social Security was not designed to be a retirement account**. It was designed to be a safety net for the elderly in an environment where many had either lost their savings or never accumulated savings (an ongoing issue since). Somewhere over the last 70 years, the narrative of social security's purpose and scope somehow changed and we lost the original intent of the program. Payments into social security are a tax and not an IRA contribution. America enacted the law to ensure our elderly would not be homeless and hungry when they were too old to work. The distinction between tax and retirement contribution is important. Many politicians stand in the way of sustainability solutions by using the argument that we are entitled to collect what we have paid in all these years, as if social security was an IRA. No politician likes to use the word, "tax". We must face the real motive behind Social Security or we will be swimming in rhetoric without a solution to this lack of sustainability. The solution is to redefine the scope of Social Security with respect to its original intent or live with eventual insolvency. No politician is prepared to be honest with the American public.

Much has changed since the enactment of the program. When Social Security was enacted the median-death age was about 65. It seemed reasonable to set the age for Social Security at 65, since only half the people would likely ever collect, and for a duration of about 9 years (the life expectancy of a 65yr old in 1935 was about 74). Now in 2015, the median death age is about 80 with substantially more than half collecting Social Security at 65. In addition, those collecting Social Security are collecting for about 18 years (life expectancy of today's 65yr old is now about 83). Our problem is an actuarial issue.

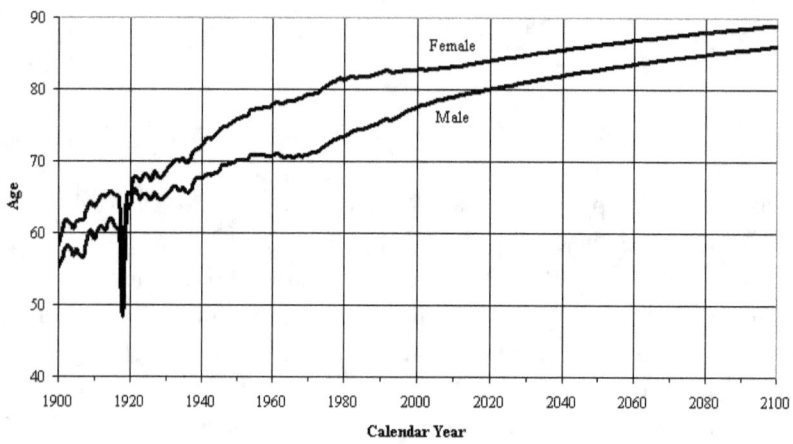

Median Life Expectancy
(Source = Social Security Administration)

This should all be good news for those of us who will live longer lives; however, the Social Security program has not kept up with the changing demographics and is no longer sustainable. This problem just gets pushed into later years where the bubble will eventually pop. The behavior mirrors the old pyramid scheme where new entrants will perpetually pay off those at the top. ALL pyramid schemes eventually collapse and this one will too. This is a political hot potato that politicians are afraid to address.

A solution to the problem needs to be proportionately shared. Here is a simple formula that gradually raises the retirement age and proportionately shares the burden.

Your new retirement age = (65 – Your_Age_Today) / 4 + 65

Your age	New Retirement Age
65	65
55	67 1/2
45	70
35	72 1/2
25	75
15	77 1/2
5	80

To the 65+ citizens currently on Social Security, you can breathe a sigh of relief. Nothing changes for you. In fact, the risk that Social Security will be taken curtailed while you are most vulnerable has greatly subsided. The program will have taken a giant leap towards solvency and you would not wake up in the next few years with a nasty surprise.

To the 55-year-old (like me), you are still getting a free ride. Even though you now must wait another 2 ½ years to retire, your longer life expectancy is well beyond what social security was intended to do for you. Be thankful that you are not bearing the brunt of the responsibility for this mess.

For the 25year old, you are likely to live a long healthy life. The good news for you is that you are not going to be the generation that will have to fund this gigantic problem when the pyramid scheme explodes. Any sharing of cost by the older generations is in your interest. If anyone is hurt by this plan, it is you, but far less than you are now. They think you are asleep since this problem is a long way off for you. I would add this cause to your list of student protests and march on Washington. Right now, you are being set to ultimately bear the brunt of this catastrophe and do not appreciate the magnitude.

For everyone, including those in the middle, you now have a "more" viable and sustainable retirement program. We all wish there were such thing as a free lunch, but the unsustainable wish fairy has been retired for some time now. If you want to get the most out of this program, you had better eat right and exercise.

Lastly, not all retirees are in the group of those who require a safety net. For the sake of solvency, does someone with enough savings to comfortably pull out $250k each year really fit the profile of someone needing a safety net? Whatever is the right threshold, a cap on eligibility must be in place. While the above prescriptions may seem unsavory to many, consider the insolvency. How long will we kick the Coke can down the road until it explodes?

Health Care Inefficiency

Health care costs in the United States are through the roof. We argue about health care premiums and ignore skyrocketing costs. The first question to be asked is if it is efficient. There is a lack of transparency. You go to the hospital to have your appendix removed in an emergency. Do you have any idea how many such operations the doctor you chose has performed or his success rate? Do you have the slightest clue what it will cost you? Why did that Tylenol pill after surgery just cost you $27? If ever there were engineered lack of transparency, it is in the health care system. I once had an MRI that cost $2,700 and I asked the radiologist exactly how much he got paid for his service. He said that he was paid $200. When I suggested that he consider purchasing a machine of his own with perhaps a few others, he said that state regulations prohibit doctors from doing so and that the state controlled the sales of the machines, probably to keep prices high. This is deliberate inefficiency by design.

Health care regulated for the wrong reasons is a form of corruption. There is seldom a free market transaction in health care and it is rife with corruption. Presumably, health care regulation is to protect us, but the costs have become so out of reach that you wonder how we are protected. Even the pharmaceuticals are in on the action. Why do Americans pay more for identical pharmaceuticals than those in other countries also supported by regulation? What is free market about that?

Unnecessary procedures are another major contributor to health care with a trickle-down effect. I once had a chronic cough and saw a doctor who gave me an $80 chest X-ray because my family has a history of lung disease. Upon review, he told me that my lungs were perfectly clear. He then offered a CAT scan if I wanted to be absolutely certain. Now I'm not sure if it was for personal profit, protection from liability or just good form. I was told my insurance would cover it but what does that do to the insurance premiums we all pay? I asked him what he would do and he told me, "You're fine, go home." If we lower the cost of healthcare, we lower premiums to affordable levels.

A volume of books can be written about this problem and the doctors themselves will tell you how the system could be fixed and improve healthcare service. Quite frankly I would not know where to start and when to finish, but there is a reason why we pay far more for healthcare than other countries. Health care is a perfect example of regulation used to corrupt. The market is not free enough and we as a nation suffer. Regulation has lost its objective; rather than protect us from corruption, it largely has institutionalized it. This is a big deal and needs to be addressed. Universal health care was one issue, but what seemed to miss the agenda were laws or the repeal of laws that would make the market freer, more transparent, and ultimately more efficient. As of 2010 we spend 2 ½ times the average of economically developed countries. Since then, the gap has grown even wider. It would be very difficult to argue that we are getting 2 ½ times better health care services in the United States. Others out there are doing a better job. Now is the time to dig in and do the American public right. We are silly and arrogant to think we have a monopoly on every good idea out there. We are smarter than that if we can just get corruptors out of the way.

US spends two-and-a-half times the OECD average

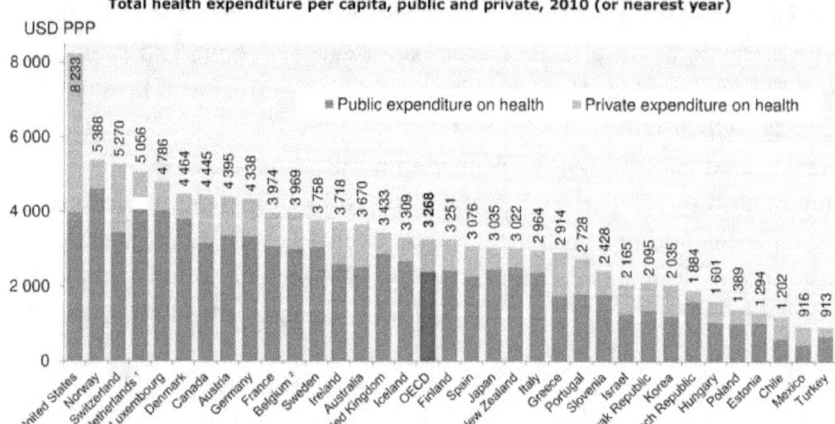

Total health expenditure per capita, public and private, 2010 (or nearest year)

1. In the Netherlands, it is not possible to clearly distinguish the public and private share related to investments.
2. Total expenditure excluding investments.
Information on data for Israel: http://dx.doi.org/10.1787/888932315602.

Source: OECD Health Data 2012.

The United States enjoys the finest doctors and research in the world. We can still maintain the high quality of our doctors and our research. Lack of transparency and free market principles threaten the quality of, and access to, health care. Doctors, hospitals, and pharmaceutical companies can charge whatever they like but the game cannot be rigged through corrupt regulation lobbied by the industry (including insurance companies and lawyers). Reducing health care costs by ½ the difference between the next highest country (Norway) or 25%, is a savings of half a trillion dollars every year and this is based on 2012 numbers. Wow! What does that do for the solvency of Medicare?

Who Pays For Our Massive Debt?

Our accumulation of debt has been used to pay for goods and services provided by both public and private entities. The capital class is anyone with savings. Those of us with savings invest our money in exchange for some rate of return. You can think of the capitalist class as a toll booth that collects money as the cars pass by. The more economic activity, the more cars pass through the toll booth, and the more wealth the capitalist class can accumulate. The capitalist class is not just some troll who lives beneath a bridge and collects tolls. What they do with the accumulated wealth is what matters. Most of the time they redeploy the capital back into the system enabling them to collect more tolls and sometimes they use the money to help others or, they use it for personal consumption.

Government deficit spending stimulates the economy and drives many cars through the toll booth and the capitalist class accumulates a lot of wealth as toll booth operators. But government had not paid for these goods and services outright. Instead they borrowed money in the form of debt via government bond issuance. The question now is who pays back the debt?

Some might argue that everyone should proportionately share the cost of repaying the debt. Others might argue that those most able to repay the debt should bear primary responsibility. If you look at who were the primary beneficiaries of deficit spending, you might point to the capitalist class but here is where some might see the waters as murky. After all, what about the average worker who received a paycheck because of deficit spending?

Ultimately, the capitalist class accumulates wealth from the labor of others. It is not wrong to do so in a free market, but it just is. In a free market, we do not want to penalize the capitalist class who adds value to our economy by helping to direct resources efficiently; however, they are certainly beneficiaries of the extra heat introduced to the economy through government spending.

All those tanks we bought during the Iraq war, all those Medicare disbursements, and all those lunches we bought for that school lunch program through deficit spending, made a lot of people very rich. Those people are the capitalist class or anyone with savings. Yet it would be wrong and would create a disincentive by simply snatching that money away from them to pay the debt. After all, it is the capitalist class whose wisdom we rely upon to allocate capital.

Here's where it gets interesting. For a long time, I felt that dead capitalists should repay the debt through a death tax. Let's go back to the cave dwellers and establish a premise.

When Gyork was banished from the hunting cave dwellers for stealing women and was accepted by the farming community, there was a very simple economy. The community grew crops and ate crops. Gyork soon learned that some in the community were either unable or unwilling to participate in farming. Those unwilling were considered to be economically immoral, as they ate more food than they were willing to produce. The village did not have the heart to see even the unwilling starve, but the village was resentful. The disabled were cut a little slack by the villagers for their condition.

The chief kept a log of a person's contribution to food production vs food consumption. When abled people died, if they had produced more than they had consumed over their life time, they were given full burial rites and buried in the field of honor, while those who consumed more than they had produced were left to rot in the field of shame. The honored farmers were revered, since they had provided for the disabled and had accumulated excess produce for the village to use trading with other communities. With the added wealth, the community could improve their infrastructure and make for a better quality of life.

While Gyork's first invention of a magic machine was not well received, he lowered his ambition and received permission to operate a machine that would do the work of twenty men making him very wealthy. Gyork wanted to leave the machine to his son when he passed and spoke to the chief. The chief explained to Gyork that in the past, villagers could pass on such wealth to heirs. At one time, a few large families ruled the village. The heirs became fat and lazy. They produced nothing and consumed off the deeds of their forefathers. Many of the heirs cared nothing about the others and squandered the wealth of their forefathers on lavish lifestyles benefiting no one in the village. The heirs had reigned for a thousand years and produced nothing. The chief put an end to inheritance and the legacy of the ruling dynasties. Gyork protested, explaining that it was his right to do as he pleased since he was the inventor of the machine.

The chief went on to explain, "When you came to the village, Gyork, you noticed that we were far more developed than the hunting cave dwellers. We taught you farming and shared our knowledge of how to make tools. Your life has become far easier since you did not have to hunt all day, traveling days away from your family. The machine you made was very ingenious, but you never would have had the time or the knowledge to make such a machine without the ancestors of the village. Your success was, in part, due to the contributions and advancements of previous generations. You have had a good life and ate as much as your stomach could hold because of your clever invention. By giving the machine back to the village, you are passing on the benefits you, too, once received. Your son will never be buried in the field of honor if he were to receive the machine. He will have no incentive to create and advance our civilization. We will never invent the TV set or ever have the chance to watch great shows like the one I have been tossing around about a talking horse. Let the machine go to the people, Gyork. It is your way to put water back into the well that you have had the privilege to drink from, yourself. It is a gift to your son to allow him to create great things by being productive and for others to improve upon what you've done. In the village, we have learned that the happiest of us are not those who eat the most, but those who have accomplished and are honored by the village forever. Do not take that away from your son. Like everyone else, you will be able to pass enough for him to have a very good life, but no more."

And this is the premise for two ideas for taxation to pay down debt. The first is to let dead people pay down the debt. They would never have become rich had they not had the platform built by generations of Americans before us, or the labor which is the ultimate source of wealth. Regardless of whether a person earned wealth with a real value contribution or obtained the wealth through some corruption, a death tax would be the great equalizer and would clean the slate. In addition, a death tax eliminates generations of unproductive heirs and power dynasties that can pay for a louder voice in politics. Heirs are not necessarily the best stewards of efficient capital allocation. The following is an excerpt from a 2014 blog posted by Bill Gates.

"I'm also a big believer in the estate tax. Letting inheritors consume or allocate capital disproportionately simply based on the lottery of birth is

not a smart or fair way to allocate resources. As Warren Buffett likes to say, that's like "choosing the 2020 Olympic team by picking the eldest sons of the gold-medal winners in the 2000 Olympics." I believe we should maintain the estate tax and invest the proceeds in education and research—the best way to strengthen our country for the future."

- *High levels of inequality are a problem—messing up economic incentives, tilting democracies in favor of powerful interests, and undercutting the ideal that all people are created equal.*

- *Capitalism does not self-correct toward greater equality—that is, excess wealth concentration can have a snowball effect if left unchecked.*

- *Governments can play a constructive role in offsetting the snowballing tendencies, if and when, they choose to do so.*

"Imagine three types of wealthy people. One guy is putting his capital into building his business. Then there's a woman who's giving most of her wealth to charity. A third person is mostly consuming, spending a lot of money on things like a yacht and plane. While it is true that the wealth of all three people is contributing to inequality, I would argue that the first two are delivering more value to society than the third." - Bill Gates

The real issue with respect to taxation is consumption of wealth and not the accumulation of wealth. Remember in the cave dweller story that economic morality was assigned to those who produced more food than they had consumed. If a farmer accumulates massive wealth but never uses it for himself, he is a hero and deserves to one day be buried in the field of honor. It makes absolutely no sense to tax income from production including labor and even wealth accumulation during one's lifetime. Consumption should be the primary source of taxation.

Cornell University's Robert Frank has long advocated for progressive consumption taxes that could do much to solve what they perceive as the ills of growing income inequality.

"Under such a tax, people would report not only their income but also

their annual savings, as many already do under 401(k) plans and other retirement accounts. A family's annual consumption is simply the difference between its income and its annual savings. That amount, minus a standard deduction—say, $30,000 for a family of four—would be the family's taxable consumption. Rates would start low, like 10 percent. A family that earned $50,000 and saved $5,000 would thus have taxable consumption of $15,000. [At 10%, he would pay $1,500 of tax].

Consider a family that spends $10 million a year and is deciding whether to add a $2 million wing to its mansion. If the top marginal tax rate on consumption were 100 percent, the project would cost $4 million. The additional tax payment would reduce the federal deficit by $2 million. Alternatively, the family could scale back, building only a $1 million addition. Then it would pay $1 million in additional tax and could deposit $2 million in savings. The federal deficit would fall by $1 million, and the additional savings would stimulate investment, promoting growth. Either way, the nation would come out ahead with no real sacrifice required of the wealthy family, because when all build larger houses, the result is merely to redefine what constitutes acceptable housing. With a consumption tax in place, most neighbors would also scale back the new wings on their mansions."

Lastly, something must be said regarding tax loopholes. If there were such a thing as welfare for the rich, it would be their ability to pay less than prescribed in taxes. If you are the working middle class, you are footing the bill for these activities. Hedge fund managers taking what should be ordinary earned income for their services but pay only capital gains tax rates, is disingenuous and wrong, though currently legal. Off-shore shell companies in countries that market themselves as secret tax havens, is also wrong, but legal. Corporate inversions and captive insurance trusts is also wrong, yet legal. The release of the Panama Papers reveals just how deep and pervasive the problem is. Adding up all the welfare fraud does not nearly compare to the welfare for the wealthy in terms of cheating on tax loopholes. At Lehman Brothers, a whole sales department was established to create non-risk offsetting trades that produced undeserved tax benefits, taking advantage of loop holes.

A major overhaul of our foreign tax treaties along with closing domestic tax loopholes would be a step in the right direction. The US can take a leadership role to end secret money funds designed to hide the wealth of thieving foreign officials, dictators, tax scammers, and money launderers. Hopefully the Panama Papers will reveal the extent of the issue. Transparency is a bummer to corruptors!

The Unemployed and Welfare

If you receive a payment from the government, you should show up somewhere and have a productive day. If you are crippled, blind, mentally challenged, with children, depressed, or out of work, there is something you can be doing to improve your life by having a productive day. All it takes is a little imagination. The work could be appropriate to your skill set, group therapy, education, training, counseling, or resume writing, but it needs to be something that you show up for to receive government assistance.

This is important for three reasons. The first is to instill an expectation that there is no free lunch and we must all contribute according to our abilities. Or at the very least, enable ourselves to do so.

Second, there is a reason someone is receiving government assistance. Perhaps learning a skill appropriate to one's limitations and circumstance will make some change. There is a far better chance for improvement with a productive day than there is by waiting at home for the check to arrive. Without some change, it would be stupid to expect a different result. A welfare state is not sustainable and the condition should be as temporary as possible. The most important reason to be productive is self-esteem and building a sense of accomplishment. While some think they would rather stay at home and watch TV, I'll bet that most would rather be productive and not be isolated in a depression trap at home.

In our culture, happiness can be defined as the expectation that things will improve in the future. That expectation is called hope. For a child, the trip to Disneyland provides more happiness than the last hour at Disneyland. Lotto winners squeal when they discover they have the winning number, but once they have assimilated their new circumstance, the money alone will not make them happy. The lotto winner still needs to believe that tomorrow will be better than today to be happy.

It is hard to fathom why we enable people at their lowest, most vulnerable state to not improve. We may as well hand them a bottle of whiskey, as we are implicitly telling them they are directionless and lost causes to be swept under the rug until they can find their own way out. They have no hope and are not vested within the larger group. They have no sense of accomplishment and are miserable. It is an invitation for any of us to corrupt.

Some grocery chains have hired the mentally challenged to do work commensurate with their abilities and these people do a fine job at what they do. It is appropriate employment with a real value-added job that does more for their happiness than the indifference society showed them before. God Bless the innovative people that implemented these programs. They are not charities. They are smart decisions that have productivised people with an economic activity validated by profit. Ask these workers if they would rather stay at home and receive a paycheck and you will hear a resounding, NO!

While there is trash on the street to be cleaned, or retirement home residents that can use a temporarily out-of-work accountant, something always needs to be done, allowing that person to allocate time to find their way back into full-employment.   Everyone should have the opportunity to lead productive lives. If they do not have the wherewithal to create productivity in their lives, then the group must step in and create productive opportunities. After all, what's the alternative?

Nanny Laws

Mayor Bloomberg was highly criticized for legislating what came to be known as *Nanny Laws*. The most talked about was a regulation against selling sodas larger than 16 ounces. If you think about it, a cigarette tax or an alcohol tax is also a nanny law. The debate centers on the right of government to decide what is in the best interest of individuals, whether they like it or not. After all, why should Mayor Bloomberg decide if I should drink a 32oz. Coca Cola or not? Does not that infringe on my personal liberty to decide for myself?

If my actions have no effect on the lives of others, government has no right to make such decisions. Recently, municipalities have looked at placing a tax of 3 cents per ounce of soda. Unfortunately, the motivation was purely to generate revenue. Of course, the soda lovers were up in arms as were the bottlers who felt workers might lose jobs. The question to ask is whether, my drinking 32oz. sodas influences others. It all depends upon if there is a tangible cost to others from my habitual desire to pound down sodas. Obesity is a health problem that costs the healthcare system in the form of indigent care. A high sugar intake contributes to obesity and increases healthcare costs to EVERYONE through higher premiums. When I develop type II diabetes and cannot afford treatment, do I have the expectation that I will be cared for? If not, then government should stay out of my business. If so, and my sugar diet does cost others, then I should pay that cost myself.

"Nanny laws" is a sarcastic term for laws that insist people pay their own way for behavior that others must otherwise pay for. Mayor Bloomberg should have taxed sugar instead of limiting purchases to 16oz. Further, they should have used the revenue to pay specifically for obesity related indigent care, unlike the municipalities that use funds for general use. These laws use the same argument for taxing negative externalities. If there were no negative externalities, government should stay out of it, but if there were, government is simply assigning costs where they belong and a tax is perfectly legitimate.

Again, the argument over soda-related jobs is a thin argument. Why should others pay for my consumption habits that knowingly cost others in terms of health care costs so that you can have a job? We all have to eat something and all that needs to be packaged and trucked somewhere. It seems there could be a job with a fruit and vegetable company or some alternative food source.

Assigning real costs where they belong is a critical decision private business makes every day and is perfectly rational to do so. Personal liberty to choose is maintained. I am free to pound big gulp sodas but I pay the cost associated with my decision. Either I will be refused subsidized health care or I will pay the tax. What makes sense about the tax is that it is embedded in the market price making it MORE of a free market transaction than if the costs were ignored. People make bad decisions all the time and do not think of consequences that affect others. A tax is the most efficient way to create free market transactions that self-regulate. The argument extends to Marijuana laws. It is far better to remove the crime element from the marijuana trade from both dealers and the penal system for offenders. Decriminalize marijuana, identify the tangible cost to society, and tax the product to pay for those consequences to society. Alcohol definitely has far reaching negative externalities and should be taxed even more.

The important point is to identify cost to the non-users and reassign the cost to where they belong. The revenues generated MUST be used specifically to alleviate the cost to non-users and for no other purpose.

Empowerment of Women

It is hard to fathom that after years of social evolution and in the greatest country on earth, we are only at the 100th anniversary of a Woman's right to vote in America. Just as amazing, is that 160 years ago, owning another human being was okay. We have improved rights and perceptions of women since then, yet today women earn 79% of a man's wage.

While I might agree that it is unfair and even wrong, equalizing violates a free market principle. The solution is never to force commerce to equalize, rather when such a discrepancy exists, to force transparency and allow the free markets to make the adjustment organically.

Imagine that states adopted a transparency law stating that each employee be given their annual wage, the wages of employees within a similar function, the wage of all employees, the wage of all males and all females. To the extent possible provide some objective metrics of employee performance including any metric requested by the employee. Then on that big day, women have enough information to decide what they will do. Smart business will recruit undervalued women and dumb business will recruit overvalued men and the gender income gap will close on its own.

Reasons may still exist why the discrepancy will never go away. Women have babies and are traditionally the primary caregiver, with a higher absentee rate when a child gets sick or mama needs to get to that midday Christmas performance, all worthy causes. This is where society can chip in, if they feel it is important enough, by enacting a working woman tax credit. It is not the job of business to make decisions that they believe to be irrational. If society wants women to have the extra time off required for family care, it is up to them to foot the bill. Mandating business to equalize will only cause business to quietly avoid hiring women.

Women are different than men and have their own unique contribution to business, government, the social fabric of our culture, and how we treat our foreign neighbors. Forced equalization under the law is important and very different than forced equalization in commerce. Support of equal rights of women is both a democratic principle and in our interest both at home and abroad.

We have a serious global population issue that is known to slow when women are empowered. A vast swath of the globe is woefully behind on the rights of women. The world would be more productive and peaceful if women's voices were heard with equal weight.

In John Gray's book *Men Are From Mars Women Are From Venus*, one of the take away points is that men have a strong urge to "become" while women have a strong urge to "belong". It would seem logical that women have a higher propensity to think in terms of group interest over self-interest and we sorely need more women leaders. Everything possible should be done to empower women, who make up half the population and have important perspectives and   contributions to make. We live on a male-dominated planet and it needs to change.

In America, we would all benefit if women played a larger role, especially black women, who are the spine of the black culture. They have filled the void as matriarchs and are eager to participate in real change.

When I say that you can't help those that do not participate in the solution, here we have a group perfectly willing to participate and can affect real change, yet we ignore them. They are so bogged down with the reality of daily survival that we are missing a huge opportunity to co-opt them towards real change!

F. Population Control

Population control is probably the most important world issue of the day and addressing it provides the greatest benefit to mankind. The chart below shows global population since 1 AD and projected into 2050. Currently, global population is over 7 Billion and we can see the changes within our own relatively short experiences on earth. Since I was born in 1960, the population has more than doubled in just 55 years. We can see the inherent stress caused on the system with global warming, food shortages, and voracious competition for natural resources.

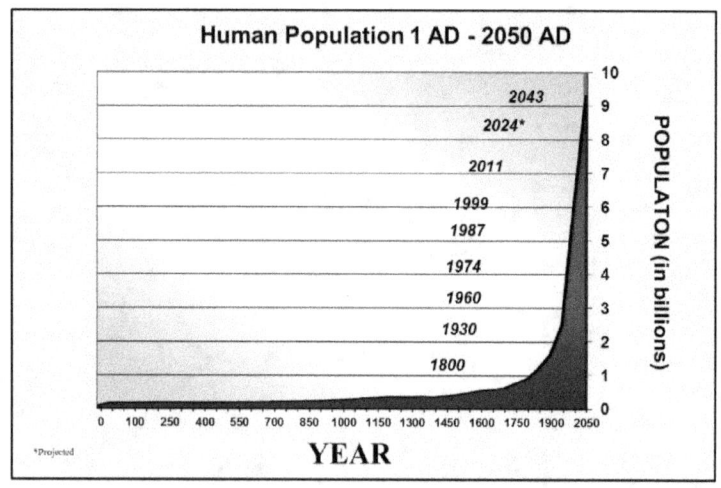

The planet's environment and resources are being strained. If we reduce the stress on the planet, trillions of us can live on this planet for billions of years. We do not have to control population but when we cross the stress threshold, Mother Nature will control it for us through war, hegemony, famine, disease, and other ugly scenarios. When Mother Nature sees disequilibrium, she is a nasty witch!

Earlier, I spoke about population in the cosmic life drama. Consider a group entity called the "human population entity." This entity has a personality, value system, beliefs, and behavior all its own, just as any individual might have. This entity is seemingly compelled to populate to its limit. When resources are ample and we have the technology to retrieve them, we will procreate like bunnies. When we sense stress, the growth rate will slow (as it has very slowly started to do, although not nearly fast enough).

If we put our fate into the hands of the Almighty, we will just close our eyes and ride it out with the faith that God will either solve these issues, or see it as an opportunity to usher in the Apocalypse. Should an Apocalypse be in the cards for us one day, I would think God does not need any help from us as bad custodians of the planet. In fact, the evil of the population entity is yet another form of our definition of corruption.

Our generation's immediate gratification of this planet by populating it with as many people as possible is more important than the future generation's enjoyment of the planet. We will elbow future generations to the rear and deprive them the enjoyment of this wonderful blue jewel we call earth. We will suck all the resources, burn all the fossil fuels into the atmosphere, and potentially create an environmental mess that Mother Nature will need thousands of years to clean up. It is not so much that the evil of this population entity's sin will destroy mankind. The corruption is not aimed at ALL future generations but is a transgression to those who will face the shock Mother Nature will bring through her wrath of war, disease, famine, and any other uglies. Human existence will likely continue after we all nuke each other. It will just take a very long pause for the radiation to decompose so that we can start the human drama all over again.

Population Decline Promotes Wealth Equality

I do not know the optimal population for the planet but would be seemingly far less than it is today. Let's imagine a target population of 3 billion people as it was in 1960. Let's further assume that it happens in the next 25 years to really amplify the effect. (I am in no way suggesting we do this so quickly because of the enormous sudden change that would be a tremendous shock, but it makes concepts easier to understand.)

Certainly, there would be less demand for resources. The current infrastructure and resource utilization matches the current quality of life on the planet. Fewer people would reduce demand and, given the supply of our time, one would expect the quality of life to go up. With half the current population, owning property, even property near the beach would be easier. We would not need to build much as we could just walk into existing unoccupied structures.

Many of the world economies are predicated on population growth, another pyramid scheme that Mother Nature will correct one day and solutions are tricky.   Asset values would fall, economies would shrink, and stock markets would drop. If social security were not already insolvent, it certainly would be under the current model given what would be a disproportionately older population.

At first, such a prospect seems like a horrible idea, but when you dig deeper, you will find an incredible aggregate benefit, even after ALL the initial repercussions. For you economists out there, dis-inflatation is different than deflation. We would seriously need to recalibrate how we think, plan, and measure prosperity. But in the end, on an aggregate level, we have the same infrastructure pie with fewer people eating it; in a macro sense fewer people would get more pie.

The issue is how do we get there, what happens during the "change phase," and the management of that change?   I remember the 2008 financial crisis where unemployment suddenly rose and asset values dropped. I likened it to the Great Depression with its similar drop in asset values and even greater unemployment. Then I asked myself, "If I look down at the big picture from 30,000ft, what has fundamentally changed from the moments preceding the crisis until the full effect of the crisis took hold? We still had the same resources, still had a skilled labor force willing to work, still had the same infrastructure, finished goods and intangibles like technology. What was so different to cause such misery?" The answer was a "dislocation shock". Nobody really knew what things were really worth and how to allocate capital because of it. The shock was caused by the absence of accurate assessment of value. Dislocation threw a wrench in the gear cogs and stopped the machine because of a precipitous change in the accounting of who owned what and who owed what. Although the machine still worked, it took time to sort things out and reassess value so that the wrench could be removed to allow the machine to run again.

America has an economic machine with an infrastructure, resources, tangible finished goods, and intangible knowledge in the form of education & technology. Reducing the population is a natural redistribution of wealth from the wealthy class to the middle and lower classes since there is less leverage capitalists have on labor. We need to seriously manage the "change phase" to minimize the dislocation shocks to the system, a big reason why it cannot be done in an orderly fashion in just 25 years.

A major problem, for the US and other economies is that they rely on growth in their models similar to the old pyramid scam of the 80's. Social Security is predicated on such a system by adding a growing population at the bottom to pay off the elderly at the top and is exacerbated by the fact that people are living longer than when social security was established in the 1930's.

How Do You Reduce Population?

I am not quite sure it can be done to an optimal level short of Mother Nature stepping in and doing it for us. However even if she did, would we only repeat the drama all over again? This is where humans can differentiate themselves from animals and plan if they choose to.

As mentioned earlier, the population entity seems to still have an appetite to grow to capacity. Slowing that train is a real challenge. It would be barbaric to mandate population control, although not doing so may be even more barbaric. The one child rule in China was a grotesque experiment in a culture that valued a male over a female child, resulting in many female abortions.

Population control can only be achieved by education, global marketing, and empowerment of women. If the population entity realized it was beyond the boundary of risk, it might back off; however, that requires creating the awareness through education. The best we can hope for is a chipping away at the psyche of the population entity. We have mass communication in a VERY BIG way. Convincing world leaders is a good start, particularly the US Congress. The US is probably the greatest beneficiary of expanding global population because we are such a large portion of the capitalist class. Larger populations provide bigger markets for us to sell into and a larger labor force is better for leveraging profit. I believe, however, that the harm, even economically, is starting to outpace benefits, even if we think in the most selfish terms.

Even if we did have the self-discipline, halving the global population to 3.5 billion, where it was in the 1970s, (just 45 years ago), the relative prosperity I project would likely encourage us to breed like rabbits all over again, unless we took even stronger effort to overcome the appetite of the population entity to procreate to its limit.

G.   Repositioning Our Economy

Technology is like water; it always wins. Have you ever had your pipes burst in a freeze? The Grand Canyon started off as a little river; now look at it! It is better to embrace, develop and export technology, than it is to try to fight it or lose our leadership role to someone else. The United States would be better served staying in front of the wave than putting our heads in the sand and later playing catch up to those that will develop a better mousetrap. By doing so, we can employ displaced workers by exporting the technology to other countries. The technology leader and exporter can create new jobs; the followers will have a much harder time making the necessary labor and wealth adjustments.

There were those that resisted motor cars. I, myself, resisted owning a mobile phone for as long as I could. Resisters have always proven to be on the wrong side of history. Technology displaces workers and there are a number of political issues to work out first, however, we should lead the world in climate control by developing alternative energy, hyper-loop trains, robotics, and driverless cars.

Often overlooked is marine technology where our research budget is a tiny fraction of space research. The oceans comprise 71% of the earth's surface. As Dr. Robert Ballard (the man who discovered The Titanic) points out, the ocean is filled with precious metals and other ample resources. Researching sea life has produced many important medical discoveries. Farming of food and possibly the farming of plants to counter the effects of global warming are all exciting possibilities with insufficient funding to develop them. Perhaps the Mariana Trench is not as sexy as colonizing Mars, but it is where we discovered important plant chemosynthesis and it is right here in our back yard.

The United States must first create the right political climate so that conservatives and liberals can have a productive discourse. After all, we need to have a game plan for the ensuing wealth inequality and labor issues that are inevitable. If we remain polarized, we will paralyze ourselves and lose our leadership role to someone else. The country that solves the social ramifications of technology and acts first, wins.

H.   Enforcement and Punishment

We have already discussed the concept of profiling and have suggested that thieves pay triple damages with a component that helps to fund law enforcement. But let us examine the policeman on the street.

Let's say I offer this job that is so deadly dangerous that you will need a gun. You will be paid $45k for starters, which is enough for a man without kids, but hardly enough to support a family. You will be allowed to take a second job to help you make ends meet, but if you are overworked and have a lapse in judgment, you could go to jail. We expect you to be kind, patient, and ignore all those experiences you have ever had that we call profiling. What do you say?

Police work should be a coveted job for those of us putting ourselves in harm's way; with a living wage and reasonable hours. This is an important job and not the place to be cheap. Police work is a psychologically demanding job and resources are required to help these men and women deal with the stress. If possible, police need to come from the communities they serve, since they understand their communities better and are less prone to misinformation that causes profiling. Police need to be measured by the overall crime health of their communities and not on number of arrests. The police and community need to be vested together and take cooperative ownership of the situation.

With respect to punishment, restitution and rehabilitation should be the primary goal when possible. Even though it feels good to watch a perpetrator suffer for their crime, incarceration alone does not serve our interest. If a convicted felon is ever eligible for release, he or she needs the skill set to succeed when released or we can expect a return visit. He may not deserve rehabilitation, but it is in our interest to provide it. Those released from prison need to belong again and become viable productive members of society or you can count on another crime and speedy return to jail.

I.   Gun Control

Recall the earlier discussion about liberals and conservatives having very different fundamental values.   Liberals value fairness and the environment they live in.   They are comfortable with change and have a general attitude that collectively we as a society can improve our conditions.   While there may be individual incidents where things do not work out the way they are planned, if society benefits in aggregate, we do it.

Conservatives on the other hand value security, order, and self-reliance. Conservatives feel more comfortable solving their own problems and do not like the idea of ceding control of their destiny to others, particularly concerning self-protection.   That one-off threat is what they feel most uncomfortable, regardless of how remote it may be. Everyone wants to feel safe and happy.   Liberals and conservatives can dismiss each other and say that the opposition is uninformed, crazy, reckless, intrusive, unpatriotic, or dangerous, but they will get nowhere.   Recognizing the concerns the opposition might be a better course of action or they can just fight it out until the winner wins; however, losers are often resentful and probably will retaliate.

The Second Amendment was enacted largely because early America could not really afford a standing army to either put down rebellion or defend our young country from foreign invaders during a time when the geopolitical environment was in a high state of flux.   It was a tradition adopted from 16th century England where the citizenry was expected and required to defend the king and homeland.   The Second Amendment also represents a theme from a world where self-reliance was necessary for survival to hostile forces, either from personal or national threats.   Self-reliance is an overarching theme of the Constitution.   The Second Amendment was appropriate for its time, but things have certainly changed since then.   The weaponry at the time was a single shot musket or revolver with the accuracy of a knuckle ball; never could the framers have imagined what technology could become.   Currently, with a standing army, National Guard, police, and state law enforcement, militias are somewhat obsolete. Did the framers intend for the right to self-protection to evolve with the unimaginable technology?   Who really knows what was in their heads at the time, but as a living, breathing document, the Constitution had provisions for change.

So here we are today. Liberals might look at the data and conclude that banning guns is rational. In aggregate, they are probably right, but that does not prevent a lone situation where someone is personally defenseless; statistics do not matter when you are at the point of a gun.

The fear of defenselessness is a real fear to a conservative and absolutely must be considered when arriving at a solution. Liberals do not feel safe with the proliferation of guns and Conservatives do not feel safe without the ability to personally defend one's self. The NRA, supported by the gun manufacturers, has stoked the fear of conservatives with a very suspicious agenda. It is both the fear of being defenseless and the fear that self-reliant rights are being taken away from them. To a Conservative, this all makes perfect sense just as Liberal logic makes perfect sense to Liberals. There is almost a religiousness to the fundamental principle that an individual must be given the freedom to solve his or her own problems and certainly not have one's personal safety depend upon others.

Unfortunately, liberals and conservatives have stopped listening to each other for some time. It is understandable that conservatives would want to draw the line for gun regulation as far away as possible when they do not trust liberals not to take away a right they feel is basic and so important. Furthermore, there is a particular ambiguity to the Second Amendment that motivates the NRA to defend a "buffer zone" (resistant to all regulation).

A well regulated Militia, being necessary to the security of a free State, the right of the people to keep and bear Arms, shall not be infringed.

The preamble is the problem. It is the only Constitutional Amendment that has the term "regulated". A staunch Liberal may want to repeal the amendment altogether, while a staunch Conservative may want to re-write it, eliminating the preamble and saying something like: *The right of the people to keep and bear arms, [evolving as the technology of weaponry evolves], shall not be infringed.* Both show complete disregard for the concerns of the opposition. "Give them an inch and they will take a mile?" This is an expression based on lack of trust and is why the two kids in the sandbox cannot seem to move the sand pile anywhere.

I, myself, am a gun owner with a conceal carry permit. When I walked into the gun store, I was greeted by NRA enthusiasts behind the desk. I knew nothing about guns, so I asked the clerk what process I should go through to responsibly own a gun. Immediately, they told me I should take a safety class to learn how to safely shoot and store my weapon, followed by a situational class to teach me how to behave responsibly and to avoid trouble whenever possible. These people respected guns and were not the Rambo types who draw their guns in a fender bender accident. They taught me a culture of respect for guns and, though it was highly encouraged, it was not a requirement. Had I wanted to, I could have purchased the gun without knowing how and when to use the power I held in my hand.

I am not afraid of these people who have taken the time to respect the power on their hips. I am not afraid for their children having an accident since their guns are religiously secured. I am afraid of the untrained anybodies who can purchase a gun at will. It is the untrained, unchecked, insane, and criminals that make the headlines and perpetuates the fear on both sides. Even the NRA would have to agree. However, the buffer mentality works both ways. Should the public become outraged enough over what is being defended in the buffer zone, they may go too far. Ironically, the NRA has put my second amendment rights at risk.

I do believe that, while understandable, the NRA is misguided with their buffer mentality pushing back against any and all gun regulation. Most Americans agree with the right to own a gun for hunting, sport, and self-protection. **The buffer zone activity is what makes the evening news and not responsible gun ownership**. The reason the NRA defends the buffer zone is because they feel the need to protect what is really important to them, namely responsible gun ownership affected by a particular weakness with the wording of the 2nd Amendment, though they may present a different face.

We see this too often in negotiations where one party makes unreasonable demands knowing that the other party will act in kind, and hope to meet somewhere on "their side" of the middle. Take for example the NRA who once supported the right to own plastic guns that were able to slip past the old metal detectors at airports. Their defense was not so much that they wanted plastic hand guns on airplanes (I would hope), but probably due to their buffer mentality to always push back on ANY and ALL gun regulation. If the NRA could keep the line of demarcation far enough away, it would be easier to defend what is really important to them. Within the current environment, the NRA is using a perfectly rational strategy, and it works.

Any credible poll will tell you that most Americans have yet to be convinced of the need to own automatic weapons and 30 round+ magazines without a background check. While at a gun show, I saw a video on YouTube of a "sliding stock AR15". For those in the trade, it is called a "bump gun". The "stock" of a rifle is the part between the trigger and your shoulder and a "sliding stock" has what you can think of as a spring. When you fire the rifle, it recoils, bouncing off your shoulder and back to your finger, forcing another discharge with no action on the shooter's part. The YouTube video showed a 100-round drum unloading in just a few seconds. A semi-automatic weapon such as an AR15 with a sliding stock is effectively a fully automatic weapon. For about $400, any criminal or mentally dangerous person could walk out of a gun show with what is effectively a high capacity fully automatic weapon and start shooting as soon as he reaches the parking lot. Background checks are not a gun show requirement. Neither side likes that idea but they have very different remedies. Liberals will want to regulate while Conservatives will buy a bigger gun to take care of their own business. The sliding stock AR-15 was designed to fill a loophole in the gun laws that the NRA supports. They will defend "bump guns" or any other firearm technology or law partly as a buffer against other restrictions. This is not an opinion, it is a fact. Ask anyone in the NRA and they will tell you it is true, however, they will vehemently disagree that regulation is the solution.

Few politicians would dare challenge the power of the NRA, even if it is not what the public consensus wants. Why does the NRA get to decide on gun laws that the majority of the public disagrees with? It is because they have power. Forget right and wrong for a moment or where you stand on the issue. They have the power and the masses do not....unless those opposed to unrestricted gun ownership form a power base stronger than the NRA. Arguing right and wrong is a waste of time. Folks like the NRA quid quo pro with politicians and ultimately politicians make the rules. Believe it or not, changing the rules of how politicians get elected and receive special interest money might be easier than changing the NRA. However, would you really expect the NRA to support anti-corruption laws that will lessen their current advantage or change their fundamental values? It is a little, *chicken and the egg.*

The power of the NRA constituency is that they are single issue voters, an enormous power that terrifies politicians. If you are leaders within the NRA, you are doing all the right things to effectively advance your agenda. You are creating incredible influence with a minority voice and getting the majority to do what they would not ordinarily do. In fact, any minority issue block should emulate your brilliant tactics. Darwin would be proud of you... until a group with greater power decides otherwise.

There are a handful of reasons why people choose to own guns, namely, personal defense, hunting, a foreign threat, a rogue government, or it is just plain fun watching a pumpkin explode. In only the rarest cases is an AR15 the weapon of choice. For home invasion, a pistol or shotgun is preferred and concealing an AR-15 when you are away from home is not practical. No self-respecting hunter ever uses a semi-automatic and even a Sherman tank won't save you from a rogue government (The siege at WACO found a stash of over 144 automatic weapons including AR-15's, AK-47's, and a .50 caliber machine gun). As for foreign threats, we have the strongest military in the world and can make an ink spot of any country we choose. That leaves recreation where big guns can be checked in or out for blasting pumpkins.

The second Amendment needs to be updated to explicitly strengthen a citizen's right to own guns apprpriate for self-protection, hunting, and sport, while at the same time allow enough regulation to keep criminals, terrorists and the mentally ill from shooting up schools and movie theaters with such efficiency. The compromise is to create enough regulation so only responsible people can own a gun but also to calm gun advocates' insecurity to defend the buffer zone that hits the evening news. Believe me I have no expectation that either Liberals or Conservatives are going to say,

"Gee, why did not we think of that before, Brilliant! – or that they will be completely satisfied.

We have a recent example in Australia of what gun regulation can do. In 1996, following a horrific mass shooting, Australia instituted stricter gun laws similar to what Americans are proposing now, namely a required license and no semi-automatics. It is been twenty years since Australians limited gun ownership and we only need to examine statistics before and after to see who is on the right side of the debate. Liberals will point to the data and gloat. Conservatives will say, I do not care about the aggregate statistics; I want to control my personal safety.

If Liberals and Conservatives do not arrive at a negotiated solution as honest brokers, then both are at risk and neither is safer. All it would take is a series of back-to-back shootings for the Liberals to have the public will to swing the pendulum too far. Ironically, gun advocates have the most to lose, even though they currently seem to control the buffer zone. In the end, we should all want and deserve both to be safer and to feel safer.

The message should go directly to gun owners and not to the NRA that is funded by gun manufacturers and will corrupt any negotiation with money. This is very difficult since so many gun owners are so loyal to the NRA. Somehow, a wedge must be created between honest brokers and the corruptors of influence.

J.   Foreign policy

Anything outside the United States must be viewed from the perspective of the American group entity with respect to policy. A major lesson we fail to learn is that foreign policy based solely on our immediate national interest, with disregard to our principles of democracy and human rights, will bite us in the fanny every time.

Democratic governments are more stable because they are less corrupt and honor human rights. Democratic governments are more predictable and are more reliable partners. Policy based on democratic principles is always in our best interest for the long term. To ever allow short term interest to trump our democratic principles is short-sighted and we have paid dearly for that mistake.

The Middle East in 90 Seconds

We laid the foundation for the Iranian Revolution when the first democratically elected leader of Iran was ousted in a UK / US supported coup. We replaced the prime minister with a dictator (the Shah), who brutalized his people, because we felt he would be a better ally in the cold war in the highly strategic oil rich Middle East. Had we the foresight, a democratic revolution that would have served our long-term interest much better. The Islamic Revolution overthrew the Shah and substituted itself as a dictatorial theocracy with the same brutalities. We did the Islamic Revolution a huge favor by giving them fodder for their propaganda. We are outraged by the hostage crisis and decide to double down. We demonstrate that we do not really care about democracy and provide armed support to Saddam Hussein so he could punish Iran for us. Now we are the Great Satan the regime labels to whip up fear in the citizenry. Remember, people who are afraid are very dangerous.

Backing another dictator like Saddam? Well, that's just backing the wrong race horse, yet again. It may have been in our short-term interest but never in our long-term interest. Of course, we all knew what happened there. The major flaw in the execution of the second Gulf War was to disenfranchise the Baathists Sunnis following military victory. We did so to teach the bastards a lesson by firing the Baathists who ran the infrastructure leaving them with no source of income. Hmm, it is no wonder we could not get the lights to work. We also disbanded the army, the country's security infrastructure, and decided they would just be unemployed. The disenfranchised Sunnis who just lost their jobs now have absolutely nothing to lose so they join up with Al Qaida and later ISIS. The point is that had we stuck to our democratic principles, we would not have blown through blood and treasure the way we did for a bad payoff.

During the Arab spring, we lost our moral authority when we supported uprisings in countries we did not like but looked the other way with respect to our allies such as Saudi Arabia and Bahrain, who brutally cracked down on any dissention. Unfortunately, the second Gulf War went over budget and weakened our will. We missed a golden opportunity to push Assad out when there was still a relatively moderate opposition and waited for ISIS to warm up to the disenfranchised Sunnis.

I once asked my friend, a Marine Lt Colonel, "How fast can you undo this policy mistake that has focused on interest over democratic principles? Does not it take time to make the shift?" His response was that we could and should do it tomorrow. He agreed there might be fallout from Arab allies, but he strongly felt the sooner the better, adding that those we think are allies are more dangerous to us than they are a help.

There is a classic corruption event going on in the Middle East. The wealth of many of these countries is predicated on the sale of oil. The revenues from the oil go to a small dictatorial leadership. The general population has been disenfranchised and they are very restless about it. These Arab leaders deflect the restlessness by pointing to Israel and then by proxy the US that supports Israel. It is the third enemy tactic used by Hitler as a premise to go after Jews. By encouraging democracy in these countries along with human rights, especially for women, we will uphold democratic principles which are in our long-term interest.

Saudi Arabia proves that we are reliving past mistakes. We consider them an important ally in the region. Ever wonder where the ideology for al-Qaida and ISIS originated? Saudi Arabia is a police state designed to instill fear that will protect the royal family. Wahhabism is the foundation for fundamentalist Islam. Wahhabism is just an ideological means to enforce a police state. Unfortunately, it uses ideology and leaks outside the borders of Saudi Arabia and causes us harm. Are the Saudi leaders really our friends? Once upon a time Saddam Hussein was our friend.

Does the US really have democratic principles or are we going to continue picking bad partners with bad habits that will bite us one day? I suppose for politicians, it is easier to kick the can down the road instead of making tough decisions.

De-corruption will create more wealth in the citizenry whereby they now have something to lose and something worth preserving. The restlessness subsides and less pressure is placed on the Israeli conflict. Less pressure on Israel alleviates fear in the Israeli government and perhaps there might even be peace one day. Further, applying democratic principles to Israel would help as well. It is in their interest to create a two-state solution as soon as absolutely possible. After all Palestinian birth rate is much higher than Israeli birthrate. The occupied territories are a heartbeat away from the South African Apartheid model and world opinion does matter. So long as the Palestinians are disenfranchised, they have nothing to lose and will remain dangerous. Provide them opportunity and hope for the future and they will have reasons to live and preserve prosperity. If the two-state solution is an ultimate objective, the whole issue of the settlements is either asinine or someone is lying.

Policy towards Non-Democratic Countries

It has been said that the first casualty of war is "the truth". Dictatorships are at war with their own citizenry. Tremendous effort is required to maintain a dictatorship because by their nature dictators are corrupt. It is by no coincidence that dictatorships limit free speech. During the 2009 student uprising in Iran protesting of rigged elections and the tossing of students off balconies by the secret police, the first thing the government did was to shut down the internet and to restrict public use of cell phones. They rounded up anyone with a dissenting voice and they disappeared forever. Given the propaganda machine against the United States, we were in a difficult situation. We were provided an opportunity to at the very least proclaim that we were in support of the democratic voice of the protestors as an act of solidarity, but we were as silent as a stone. Somehow, we allowed whatever short term interest argument to interfere with our democratic principles. With such a conflict of interest verses principle, we shout to those who might rise for the cause of democracy that we are an unreliable partner.

What I would have loved to see was a gift from the sky courtesy of USA. It would not have been bombs or propaganda leaflets; it would have been millions of highly encrypted smart phones floating down on little parachutes, each with independent service that enabled protestors to communicate with one another, post videos, and organize. Dictators hate transparency. Citizens can be far more influential than a foreign army, a lesson to remember.

New technologies exist called "mesh networking", where any Bluetooth device can daisy chain a private network completely OFF the internet grid. At first blush, this may seem like another social media gimmick; however, this technology is a real game-changer. Mesh Networking was used during protests in China, where private networks were created off the internet grid and were uncontrollable by the Chinese government. This could be a huge foreign policy tool that is more effective than bullets. Had we air dropped these little gifts, the Ayatollah would have crapped his britches, since corruptors hate transparency and we would have shown solidarity with the democratic movement.

Another lesson from the Arab Spring is that, for democracy to take hold, the citizenry needs to be the front line of the fight and spill its own blood. The Iraq and Afghan wars were not organic wars of the citizenry to achieve their own democracy. The citizenry simply got caught up in a war of governments and the victor decided to implement democracy whether they wanted it or not. They were forced, as pawns of a global chess game, to spill blood for a cause that was not their own. This is why democracy has yet to really take hold in those countries after more than a decade. It is why we were so surprised that Iraqis were not more appreciative for setting them free by cheering us in the streets. We only managed to create a power vacuum since the displacement of Saddam had no determined democratic movement to replace him. The resulting vacuum was replaced by an American picked regime with no determined citizen support and a new class of disenfranchised Baathists and soldiers. Because they were not ready for democracy and hadn't earned it, the Saddam vacuum was a perfect breeding ground for the dictatorial regime of ISIS. A similar outcome occurred in Afghanistan where a corrupt government could deliver neither security nor infrastructure. The Taliban continued to nip at the heels of democracy and, because the citizenry never had an organic movement towards democracy, they did nothing to stop it. Democracy was just some outside bloody do-gooder's dream.

In Egypt, on the other hand, the protest was more organic. Students frustrated with unemployment and human rights abuse wanted more democracy and went to the streets to oust Mubarak, whose corruption squashed opportunity and violated their human rights. When Mubarak was replaced by an elected leader from the Muslim Brotherhood, he proved to be no different than his predecessor as far as the citizens were concerned. Because Egyptians spilled their own blood in the first protest, they took right to the streets again to make yet another change. They were determined because their own blood was shed for their organic cause. This is a key ingredient when we decide to help others in their quest for democracy. Of course, Egypt has more work to do but they have the right foundation for future change that will take time. We can help, but they need to do the heavy lifting, otherwise democracy will never take hold.

The last lesson is my view that everyone loves a soldier and nobody likes an occupying cop. The first lesson in war is that a large part of a battle is choosing your battlefield. Our competitive advantage is in fighting a lightning fast high tech war that completely overwhelms any opponent. The United States is at a competitive disadvantage when it comes to occupation. The front-line fight must always be done by those who have the most at stake, supported by coalition technology, and led by the US for the cause of democracy. A group coalition of nations is always stronger than any single nation. The United States should always be prepared to lead, but if there is no will from coalition governments and no will of the citizenry towards fighting for their own freedom, the United States should stay out of the fight. You cannot help those that do not participate in the solution. Sadly, you can only watch them suffer. This is a cruel truth that we should post on the world bulletin board so that everyone knows where we stand.

While I support the efforts of the UN, it may not be the best vehicle to promote freedom and democracy. What gives the right for corrupt non-democratic countries to have a full seat at the table? Why do China and Russia have veto power on the Security Council? It is time to set up a league of democratic countries to promote democracy around the world using diplomatic and economic influence. NATO countries might be the better vehicle if it included an economic policy and a mandate to promote democracy. Shrinking a bad guy's wallet can have more effect than punching him in the face. We need to choose our battlefield and our economic influence gives us home field advantage, especially if we have the power of a group behind us. The United States simply does not have the resources to be the world protector. Without the power of a larger group with shared interest, it will only be a matter of time until we deplete our resources and lose our ability to create a safer global neighborhood. Before we try to de-corrupt foreign countries, we should de-corrupt ourselves as a model to others so that we can reclaim moral authority.

China and North Korea

With any adversarial relationship, you have a handful of choices. Either you can fight, accept by doing nothing, or negotiate. But before we do anything, SunTzu would advise us to "know thy enemy".

China, for the longest time, was a third world country with a cheap source of labor. As the barriers of world trade broke down, companies flooded to China for their cheap source of labor. While they hold a mountain of cash, it is mainly in the foreign currencies of countries that have purchased from them. There are only three things you can do with a foreign currency. You can invest it in foreign bonds or hard assets of that other country (like real estate, or businesses so long as you are allowed to do so), you can buy goods and services, or you can trade it for another currency. Ultimately, you must purchase something denominated in that currency. This gives us more power than we might realize.

China eliminated environmental regulations to further grease the wheels ignoring an enormous cost that they have been accreting all these years. Their economy is notoriously rife with corruption. The solution for them is to artificially inflate their markets and to expand unethically to acquire wealth from other nations. There tactics are corrupt and dangerous.

China does not seem to really understand what it means to be a free market economy. They desperately rely on an unsustainable growth trajectory to hide the mismanagement of their economy. China is building a house of cards that is destined to collapse. Instead of getting back on track using sound free market principles, China is looking for alternative sources of growth by bullying the neighborhood. China is propping up its house of cards, by trying to expand unearned influence in the Pacific Rim. Parallels can be made between China Imperial Japan prior to the war. Their biggest obstacle is the United States and we must show China a way to alleviate their precarious position without bullying their neighbors.

North Korea is a problem for everyone including China. A free North Korea is in the interest of China as another potential market to sell into with a competitive Chinese advantage. Instead, China is in the position of subsidizing North Korea with the short term goal of avoiding disruption and a potential refugee crisis. North Korea is creating fear amongst its neighbors and people who are afraid are dangerous. One false move by the crazy fat boy and even China is in big trouble. China is beginning to realize that the dust they have been sweeping under the carpet is about to have its day of reckoning. China must be convinced that it is in their interest to resolve the matter and quickly.

In the meantime, South Korea and Japan need to make a serious decision since they will bear the brunt of North Korean aggression. This is a threat that is headed in one direction. Do these countries have the resolve to take the risk now when consequences are less than they will be in the future? It is a game of chicken; who will blink first? One would think that a high probability head shot against Kim Jong Un is in order. Incentivizing the Chinese might be the answer. If NATO democracies exerted economic influence, China might be more easily convinced.

Up until now, North Korea has fulfilled its principle goal of keeping the regime in power. The regime's principle goal has never been the welfare of its people. The deification of Kim Jong Un must be destroyed. With a brainwashed Kamikaze citizenry, this is very tricky business. China is definitely in the best position to pull this off or at least to create enough threat to worry Kim. He does not want to die, and if he were ever to be convinced to back down, China can do it. It is time to take a stand.

Allowing North Korea to further develop its program is not an option.

The key to beating North Korea is to beat Kim Jong Un's strategy. The glorious leader surrounds himself with 3 million privileged supporters in Pyongyang that live in a comparative Disneyland compared to the 21MM starving North Koreans outside Pyongyang. Everyone is scared to death of the police state. The key to unlocking power is to undermine trust amongst those in Pyongyang and to spread the truth to those with little to lose because they are starving. Breaking the control Kim has over his people is more effective than facing off with an army. We have seen this clever strategy used by the Russians who create discord amongst democratic nations with fake news. In this particular case, we are debunking the regime's propaganda machine with facts. Chip away at the cooperation that the police state relies upon. Weaken the enemy without firing a shot. Perhaps we air drop smart phones onto the countryside that can communicate off the grid. Set them up with videos to entertain, educate, communicate and hopefully organize.

Do not think that glorious leader would not crack down, but it takes enormous resources that North Korea can't afford. I would not expect a victory with this strategy alone, but it would definitely degrade the power of the regime.

When all else fails, it is time for a stiffer response. As an armchair military tactician with zero experience, I would try to negotiate but with a clear goal of de-nuclearization. If negotiations fail, destroy their navy especially the submarines that are the unpredictable delivery system. In addition, submarines are probably how North Korea would transport nuclear material to our enemies. It is far less personal than a land attack and is currently the greatest threat to the United States and their allies.

Russia and Syria

Russia, has similar imperialist aims, though they seem less to do with economics and have more to do with the goals of one man trying to mask his failures to improve the lives of Russian citizens. Putin's aim is to benefit the oligarchs of Russia who empower him. His goal is to retain power. Whipping up a little nationalism by invading nearby countries works for Vladimir Putin, but it reverses the development of democracy and is very destabilizing, corrupt and dangerous.

Putin is cleverly using the tactic of creating disunity in democratic countries.   The tactic is genius, effective, cheap and dangerous. Democratic countries need to understand him and beat his strategy. His vulnerability is that he is overextending himself. Over-extension failed Russia during the Cold War and in Afghanistan. It failed the U.S. in Viet Nam and the recent Middle East wars. The democratic countries of NATO can do more with their wallets than they can with their missiles.

The key is to make bad behavior very expensive for uncle Vlad. His intrusion into Ukraine and Syria is very expensive but we can make it even more expensive for him. Hegemony ultimately requires an economic payoff or it only weakens the bully. What Putin fails to realize is that he had better think twice about what he asks for because he just might get it. It is very expensive to govern those that resist. The irony is that the more successful he is achieving influence over the unwilling, the weaker he becomes.

As for Syria there are three belligerents - - the Assad Regime, ISIS, and moderate rebels. Russia must know that no long term solution can exist with a dictator who is responsible for a half million casualties (2% of the population) and 4MM refugees (17%).   We can either step back and watch Putin drain his coffers or create a sequential (and private) strategy to cooperatively defeat ISIS and then offer Assad a plane ticket to live the rest of his life in a Crimean Villa. The Syrians must determine how they are governed otherwise Russia will deplete its resources by propping up Assad forever. The Western democracies can demonstrate their determination to make that very expensive for Putin by weakening his support base with more targeted sanctions. Putin needs a golden bridge to extract himself from the unsustainable path he is on. He needs to be convinced in a way he can save face.

Just as Putin created a brilliant strategy to get democracies to fight amongst themselves, we too, can create alternative strategies that are far cheaper and more effective.

For both Russia and China, we cannot only make their bullying behavior expensive to weaken them, we can improve our own power by strengthening our own economy. To solve health care, social security, deficit spending and to create social harmony within the United States is very bad for these two adversaries. It expands our potential and the influence of our wallets. Depolarizing and de-corrupting America is very bad for China and Russia. It is probably the best long-term strategy to improve our own national security.

Conclusion

Corruption is the root of all that is evil in the world. Corruption in many ways is the definition of sin, itself. We often focus on the wrong issues attacking those who seem guilty by association like the demonized 1%, or even individual politicians. The enemy is corruption and the head of the snake is a corrupt political group entity. Unless we eliminate corruption by those making the rules, I would have to use my father's adage, "We are peeing up a rope." We are at a crossroads where the prize is an America without corruption. Most of our economic and social problems evaporate in the absence of corruption. Yes, it is idealistic and utopian, but anything that moves us closer in that direction is an improvement.

With the recent development of the internet, we live in an exciting time. We can make a giant leap in social evolution and the potential prize is really exciting. We have so much potential right now it is mind blowing. We can create a better society for ourselves and hopefully for the world at large.

I do not claim to have a monopoly on truth. I'm just an ordinary guy with a few quirky ideas. I think corruption can be defeated with a clear objective and a clever strategy. I am absolutely positive there are some readers far more creative and smarter than myself who can come up with better ideas and strategies to move us closer to de-corrupting the world we live in. I only hope that my humble contribution here will get us talking, coalescing into a determined group, and acting towards an action plan to develop an Independent movement of true patriots who are tired of bitching around the water cooler. Start the dialogue. The hand of God won't come down to rescue us. He does not seem to do those sorts of things. It is up to us to create the world we want to live in.

www.ingramcontent.com/pod-product-compliance
Lightning Source LLC
Chambersburg PA
CBHW071350280526
45787CB00001B/280